Investing:
Invest Like a Pro

Stocks, ETFs, Options, Mutual Funds, Precious Metals, and Bonds

5th Edition

By

ALAN ANDERSON

Alan Anderson

© Copyright 2017 – All rights reserved.

Alan Anderson

author is not engaging in the rendering of legal, financial, medical, or professional advice.

Table of Contents

Introduction

Investing money in the stock market is possibly the best way for a person to increase his or her monthly income. Such investments are better known as portfolio investments, and, depending on where you put your money, you will receive dividends, payouts, returns or interest. However, the mere thought of investing in a volatile market scares many people, most of whom prefer to choose safer investment options, such as bank accounts and government bonds.

However, these do not pay a good rate of interest, and, just by choosing to put the money into the share market, a person can increase its value several fold, but getting this person to take up stock market investments may be a difficult task. More than volatility, it is the lack of proper knowledge that scares people away. Thus, the need of the hour is to educate potential investors on the basics, and give them a good idea of what it takes to invest in the share market.

To help with this process, this book will guide you through the basics of stock market investments and teach you how you can wisely invest and increase your money's worth. There are separate chapters dedicated to understanding the different forms of investment options that are available and how you can smartly invest in them.

I thank you for choosing this book. I hope that you enjoy reading it and that it succeeds in teaching you a thing or two about stock market investments.

Alan Anderson

Chapter 1: Investment Basics For Beginners

In this chapter, we will look at stock market basics and other important information that you have to understand before you start investing.

What is the Stock Market?

The stock market refers to a place where buyers and sellers converge to trade securities. These securities can take the form of stocks, shares, bonds, options, etc., all of which belong to companies. The stock market pools together all of these securities and assists buyers and sellers in buying or selling them to make a profit. These securities can either be listed in the stock exchange or traded privately. Any market that lists stocks and other securities is known as a stock market. The exact place where the trading takes place is known as a stock exchange.

Within the stock market, there are different types of markets in which a person can invest. These markets are different aspects of the stock market, and they serve different functions. Although certain functions may overlap, there is a defining characteristic that separates them. The most important ones are the equity and share markets.

What is the Equity Market?

The equity market is part of the stock market. While the stock market itself deals with both private and public stocks, the equity market only deals with public stock. This public stock is usually referred to as equity interests, where people can buy and sell the stocks of a publicly traded company. This type of stock is usually traded and sold in either the stock exchange or over-the-counter. In fact, equity is the technical term for what everyone thinks of the stock market – the selling and buying of stocks of various companies.

This market is one of the most important in the stock market, as it is at the heart of a free-market economy. As a tradeoff, companies make a profit for being in the stock market while giving investors a small share of ownership of a given company. The amount of a company you own depends on what percentage of stocks you own.

What is the Share Market?

Although most people use the terms "stock market" and "share market" interchangeably, they are not the same. The stock market incorporates the trade of all types of securities, encompassing bonds, options, futures and debentures, ETFs, etc., whereas the share market only deals in shares. These shares belong to companies, which list them for people to buy and sell with the aim of contributing towards the company's upkeep. The majority of people invest most of their money in shares as opposed to the other types of securities. Share markets are extremely volatile as compared to stock markets.

The similarities between equity and share markets are the reason why many confuse the two, as you can buy shares in an equity market. However, the main difference is that an equity stock holder is a person who owns stock in any company, while a shareholder is a person who owns shares in a specific company. Both types refer to owning stocks and shares, but one is more particular than the other.

Where are the Stock Exchanges?

There are several stock exchanges around the world, as each country needs one. There was a time when there was just one, that is, the Amsterdam Stock Exchange, which is the oldest stock exchange in the world. It dates back to 1602 and was set up by the Dutch East India Company. Subsequently, the New York Stock Exchange came into being, and it is the biggest stock exchange in the world. The Bombay Stock Exchange was the first one to be set up in Asia and is said to be one of the most affluent in the world. There are many others all around the world, and they comprise the physical stock exchanges. Apart from these, there are online stock exchanges like the NASDAQ, which allow people to trade independently.

These independent stock exchanges have a special name. People call the independent exchanges the over-the-counter market, and, like the stock exchanges, over-the-counter markets can be based anywhere in the globe.

What is the Over-The-Counter Market?

Over-the-counter (OTC) markets are like a stock exchange but do not have set locations and are completely decentralized. As mentioned earlier, OTC exchanges are completely independent, and dealers can buy and exchange anywhere. Stocks and shares are sold and bought through different means, such as by phone, emails or online. OTC markets are mainly used to trade such stocks as bonds, derivatives, currencies, etc. However, people can and have traded equities on this market. An example of this is OTC QX.

There are two different types of clients in an OTC: a "customer market" where brokers trade with their clients, which include corporations and institutions, and an "interdealer" market, which refers to dealers trading with each other. Dealers in an OTC will set their own prices in the market, and prices and quotes for stocks differ from each dealer. Thus, it is better to shop around for a deal.

It is very risky to deal in OTC markets as they have fewer regulations, even though in recent years, there has been an effort to make the OTC markets less dangerous.

What are Primary and Secondary Markets?

Markets are of two types, namely, primary and secondary markets. Primary markets are those in which companies declare initial public offerings. These are mostly offered to the affluent or to the employees of a company. These shares are then traded in the secondary market, as they are no longer primary and are preowned or used stocks.

Stock exchanges are secondary markets, as they deal in stocks that are bought and sold multiple times, and they don't have direct access to the primary stocks. Most regular trade transactions take place in the secondary market. Many people have access to these markets, and they interact with other buyers and sellers to conduct their trade.

An example of a primary market is when a company first goes public and starts selling stocks and shares. This moment is called an initial public offering, commonly referred to as an IPO. IPOs are only sold in the primary market. If someone sells their stock from an IPO and some else buys it, this is an example of the secondary market.

Who are Brokers?

Brokers are people who help commoners buy and sell stocks on the stock market. They assemble on the floor of the stock exchange and buy and sell shares on behalf of their clients. They are the intermediaries who help keep the system moving forward. There was a time when these brokers would assemble on the floor and shout at the top of their voices to buy and sell these stocks, but since the nineties and the emergence of computers, the system has changed, and they now communicate through connected computers.

Back in the day, only the rich could afford to hire brokers and deal in stocks, but now, anybody interested in trading can do it with considerable ease. You have to be a member of the stock exchange in order to trade, and given that these brokers represent companies that are members, you can trade through them. Brokers usually charge a small fee for their services.

It is important to remember that a broker is different from a dealer and financial advisor. Unlike a broker, a dealer is someone who buys and sells for his or her own gains. It is possible for someone to be both a broker and dealer for his or her firm; such people are unsurprisingly called broker–dealers. Meanwhile, a financial advisor is not a broker or a dealer who is licensed to work in exchanges and has a firm to back him or her up. A financial advisor cannot sell or buy stocks for clients. A financial advisor is a money expert who deals with mortgages or tax advice, although an advisor does not need to be licensed to work. However, a financial advisor can advise a person on whether he or she should have invested in the markets or not based on his or her financial situation.

While people do use the terms "broker" and "trader" as synonyms, as stated above, a broker is a licensed sales agent while a trader, on the wishes of a portfolio manager, just buys and trade stocks. However, the jobs of a broker and a trader are similar, as they buy and sell securities for their clients, whether the clients are average persons or corporations. The main difference between the two is that a broker is in direct contact with his or her clients while a trader is not. This is important to remember when choosing help to buy and trade stocks.

What is a Demat Account?

There was a time when companies would issue physical certificates (carrying their name and the buyer's name) to the buyers of their stocks, and the buyers would have these framed and placed in their homes. If they were to sell their stocks back, they had to give the certificate back to their broker, who would then find a buyer for it and, once the sale was done, would collect the money and remit it to the original seller. All this would take weeks, which would amount to a small loss for the seller. However, it is now possible to buy and sell stocks in a matter of minutes, thanks to the Demat account. The Demat account refers to dematerialization and is meant to do away with physical certificates. The broker maintains a digital copy of the share's documents and trades it in lieu of the client. The Demat account is where you log in to check your balance and your complete investment portfolio. If you wish to know how much you have in investments, then you will be asked to punch in your user identity and your password, which will be unique to you. You will also have the chance to maintain a soft copy of your account, which your company will mail to you.

A great benefit of a Demat account is that you avoid the risks associated with physical securities, such as stock theft and losing certificates. Demat accounts can also cut extra costs because they are digital, not physical, so you avoid paying for costs like handling and stamp duty that you would otherwise pay for if you had a physical certificate. Moreover, risks are lower because an electronic certificate is difficult to fake, and there is no chance for the certificate to be damaged during delivery. Furthermore, everything is done in one account, which makes it easier to keep track of all your investments.

Why Do Shares Fluctuate?

The share market works on the basic principle of demand and supply. When there is a lot of demand for a stock, the stock's value will rise. This is because there are limited stocks and many buyers. Thus, given that not all can buy the remaining stocks, only the best of the lot will be able to do so. On the contrary, if there is a lot of supply for the stock, then the market value will come down because of the excess supply and low demand. This is what causes the fluctuations in the market value of stocks. Such demand and supply are governed by the progress of the company and how they are doing financially at any given point. Apart from this, there are many other factors that determine share price fluctuations. It all depends on how the market will react to certain elements that are present both internally and externally. These fluctuations are beyond the investor's control, and the price differences are seen as market risks.

An example of this would be a large number of people investing in Apple, which would cause the stock to drop. This is why there are ways to make stocks that are in high demand available at certain times. This will be explained more in a later chapter.

What are Dividends?

Dividends are profits that are paid to shareholders by the companies whose shares they hold. As previously mentioned, depending on how well a particular company is doing, people will invest in their shares and have a share in their profits. Thus, if they are making a huge profit, they will be more than happy to share it with their shareholders. This is mainly for long-term investors who hold on to shares for long periods of time. However, you must remember that this is not a consistent return on your investment, and you will not get a dividend all through the year, year after year. You will possibly get two or three dividends a year if the company is good and doing well for itself. There are, however, some companies that consistently declare profits and also dividends for the shareholders. These companies will issue something known as bonus shares as well, which can also be classified as dividends. So if you were to hold 500 shares of Microsoft, and they decided to split the shares into two, then you would receive bonus shares, and your total Microsoft holding would become 1000 shares.

While dividends may be a sign that a company's growth has stopped, it also shows that the company has money to give back to investors. This is why dividends are great because they show a company's success, given that the more money a company makes, the more they have to give as dividends. This is also why dividends are reliable; it is very difficult for companies to fake it, as they either have money or they don't. Dividends are also great to invest in during a recession, as they are not as volatile as stocks. This is because dividends are shares.

What Types of Investors are there?

There are two types of investors who usually take part in stock exchanges, namely, long-term investors and short-term investors. Long-term investors are those who invest in bulk and invest for long periods of time. They are concerned about the dividends that they will receive and not really bothered by the growth in the face value of the share. Short-term traders are those who will buy and sell shares on a daily or weekly basis, and they wish to earn profit from the fluctuations in the face value of the share. There are also midterm investors who can hold shares for a month to six months.

Anyone can become whatever kind of investor they want to be. However, it is better to conduct research on the different types and see which one suits you and your investment ideas. More on this is explained in Chapter 2 of this book.

What are Sectors?

Every stock market has thousands of shares that are listed by hundreds of companies. If they are not sorted out, then it will get extremely confusing. Therefore, they are classified under sectors, which pertain to their individual line of business. For example, the banking sector lists all the banks that have their stocks listed on the stock exchange. Similarly, there is the IT sector, the pharmaceuticals sector, the fast-moving consumer goods sector, etc. You can choose to follow any one of these sectors or many of them at any one time.

Sectors make it easier to find stocks because you just need the sector information to look for the stock you want. Other investment markets also have their own sectors. For example, real estate has its own sectors, which are important to those who invest in real estate properties. These sectors include commercial and residential properties.

Should I be an Expert to Trade?

No. Although having in-depth knowledge is always a good thing, you need not be a market expert to trade. You will have a broker to assist you, and all you have to do is keep an eye on your stocks. Once you get the hang of it, you will know how to trade independently and make smart choices for you and your investments. Until such time, you will have to rely on a broker, who will tell you where to invest your money. If you think you can make an independent choice, then the option to buy and sell will be provided to you.

It is important to conduct research once you get started, as this makes it easier for you to trade independently. However, you may be able to avoid high broker commission fees once you feel comfortable independently making stock choices, as you will no longer need a broker that also gives financial advice. We will learn more about this later.

Are There Risks Involved?

Yes. Nothing in this world is free from risk, and the stock market is no different. There are a lot of risks involved in investing in the stock market, and the degree of risk differs from security to security. Although there is no guarantee that any one form of security is low on risk and high on profits, it is possible to choose options that will yield bigger profits while minimizing risk. You can choose where to invest your money depending on how much risk you are willing to take, and remember: no risk, no gain.

When is the Best Time to Start Trading?

It depends on what you want to invest in. If you just want to invest in short-term stocks, then you can do it at any point, given that there is no minimum age for an adult to start investing his or her money. You just need to have the minimum amount of money to start a brokerage account.

However, there are some who believe that the younger you are when you start trading in the stock market, the more you make in a lifetime. While that can be true, it does not consider the risk factor and who is investing in riskier stocks, bonds, etc.

Long-term investing is different, as it is dependent on what you are investing. For example, a young woman setting up a retirement fund is more likely to receive more dividend payments than a woman who started her retirement fund later in life. However, keep in mind that not all long-term investments are the same, as you will see later with bonds that investors can set up to mature years in the future.

Are Shares and Stocks the Only Types of Investments?

No. Apart from these, there are many other forms of investments that you can choose from. These include options, ETFs, bonds, mutual funds, etc. All these are better known as financial securities. Depending on the investment options that you have and the money that you wish to invest, you can diversify your portfolio and incorporate as many of these into it as you like. Each of these will be explained in detail in the chapters to come, and you will gain thorough knowledge on each aspect by the time you are done reading.

Chapter 2: Investing In Stocks And Options

In the previous chapter, we looked at the basics of stock and share markets. Now, we will look at what stocks and options are and why you should or should not invest in them.

What are Stocks?

Stocks are also known as shares and are issued by companies to the public. All companies need to remain open and have enough money to function on a day-to-day basis. This is not possible if the company relies on its profits alone; it needs help from a lot of people. This monetary help is availed by issuing shares of the company. When a person buys a share of a company, then he or she has a share in the company's profits and losses. This means that this person is a part owner of the company, and such ownership pertains to the amount of shares that he or she holds. So say, for example, you hold 2000 shares in Microsoft out of 100,000 shares; then you become a 2% owner of the company. However, remember that this is just an example, and Microsoft will have a lot more shares than that. Thus, you might end up becoming just a 0.2% owner. You will be paid either a 2% or 0.2% dividend depending on your investment.

Choosing the best shares depends on whether you want to be a long-term investor or a short-term investor. If you are in for the dividends, then choose companies that are well reputed and are known to pay good rates of dividends. If you are looking for short-term investments, then look for stocks that are priced between $5 and $15 and have a percentage change of between 1 and 10%.

Getting Started with Stocks

Stocks may seem to intimidating for those who have never invested. However, there are some basic things to understand before you invest. The first thing you should do is invest in a company you know. Given that many corporations are a part of the stock exchange, it should not be hard for you to buy stock.

For example, if you are a big fan of Disney, you should start out by buying some stock in the company. This way, stocks seem less intimidating, as you are buying from a brand you recognize.

However, you should be wary of risky stocks during your first time investing. For example, you should not buy stocks from a social media company, as these types of stocks are extremely risky, and you will learn why later in Chapter 5.

Another rule of thumb about stocks is to avoid what you don't understand. For example, if someone – a friend or your broker – is trying to get you to invest in a stock option but you don't understand it, do not invest in it right away. This is why you should always conduct independent research so you can know when to invest and when not to invest. The stock market might have a large number of advantages, but it has some significant disadvantages as well. This chapter will help you understand some stock basics.

Advantages of Investing in Stocks

The advantage of investing in stocks lies in the fact that companies will pay out a certain amount of dividend each month. This is only for long-term investors. If the company is good enough, then they will consistently pay out dividends, but this will entirely depend on how they are faring financially. So to make the best of your investments, conduct fundamental research before choosing companies. This involves looking at their total value, their debts, how much dividend they have paid in the past, how regularly they pay, etc. All of these will have an impact on the amount you will receive as profit.

Short-term and medium-term investors do not receive dividends, but they can make a profit from their investment sooner, as they do not have to hold on to the investment for years just to see a return. This is the advantage that these investors have over long-term investors. However, it is important to figure out whether you want a see a return in less than 10 years or whether you want monthly dividends.

Another advantage of stock investment is that if the economy is great, you can take advantage of the growth of corporations. Given that more consumers are spending, companies make more money, and you will receive a higher dividend. Short-term investors can make money quickly as long as they follow trends and know when to sell and buy. Another thing about stocks is that they are easy to buy and sell. You can buy stocks online or via a broker or financial advisor.

Alan Anderson

Disadvantages of Investing in Stocks

The disadvantage of investing in stocks is that there are no guarantees. You are not guaranteed that you will get back what you invested, and there is no guarantee that you will receive a monthly dividend. The company will decide whether they wish to give away a dividend or not, and you can't hold it against them if they decide not to. Although preference shareholders are promised a certain sum as fixed dividend, which they will receive every month, common stockholders don't have this privilege. Moreover, it is not easy to get your hands on preference stocks unless you work in the firm or are extremely affluent.

Common stockholders get their stocks from the secondary markets, as they do not have easy access to the primary market. While common stockholders do not get the special perks of being a preference shareholder, they can still take advantage of some of the profits from the stock, as they can sell when the price rises and buy when the prices are low. This means common stockholders will make a profit but not as much as preference shareholders.

Another disadvantage is that it takes a large amount of time. To be successful, you have to conduct research on every company and decide whether or not you think the stock is profitable. Moreover, regular stockholders (those who hold common stock) – those who are not bondholders or preferred stockholders – are paid last if the company becomes broke. Another thing to remember is that you compete against professionals, such as institutional traders who have an advantage over you.

How Does the Stock Market Operate?

The stock market functions in a fairly straightforward fashion. There are not too many factors that affect its functioning, and it is more or less like the purchase and sale of products in the market.

For example, a new product arrives on the market. It is obvious that people will want to purchase it and be among the first ones to have it. However, after using it for a long time, they will either throw it away or give it to someone else.

Stocks or shares can be compared to these products. For example, Microsoft has announced good results. Everybody will want Microsoft shares and will start buying them rapidly. This will cause a sharp rise in its price per share. This is a good thing for all those who are already holding on to their shares, as the face value will double or triple. Now, it is an existing shareholder's choice to sell back his or her shares in the market and earn a profit or to hold on to these shares and not sell them. If a large number of holders do decide to sell, then the value of the stock can drop. Although there will be a lot of buyers interested in buying, there might be an excess of sellers and fewer takers. Thus, the face value might end up dropping. However, if the majority decides to hold on to it and not put it out into the market, then it will work to the existing holders' advantage, as there will be more takers and fewer sellers, which will help the price shoot up.

It is generally hard to predict who will sell and who will not. Although an experienced trader will be able to point at the number of people who will sell their stocks and the number that will hold on to it, it is difficult to arrive at exact numbers. So the most you can do is gather experience and write down market trends to see when it is ideal to buy and sell stocks.

This is better known as timing the market. An inexperienced trader will panic at the slightest drop in prices and not know when to hold on and when to sell. He or she will end up selling a lucrative stock short and then realize a loss on profit. This means that this person will not make full use of the stocks that he or she is holding and will end up selling it at a time when its price is consistently rising.

Knowing how to time the market is crucial for any trader. Ideally, it is best to buy stocks when they have dipped and then accumulate further when they rise and dip again. There is no point in buying today, allowing it to rise, see a dip approaching, and selling it short. A good trader will stay away from such trading. For example, it is a good idea to buy a stock at $50 and then wait for it to rise to at least $150, and if it happens to dip to $75, then that is the time to accumulate more instead of selling the stock. However, if you think you would like to move away from the stock at the $150 mark and not reinvest in it for some time, then it is a wise choice to exit on it at that particular point.

If you think you are capable of trading on a daily basis, then there is no harm in trying it. This is better known as intraday trading. Intraday trading is said to be a very risky business but, if you are an experienced hand, then you will know that everything in the stock market is risky, so why not indulge in some quick money-making activities and forgo waiting long periods of time to see results?

Intraday trading refers to the buying and selling of stocks on the same day. If you buy by 10 a.m. today and sell it by 2 p.m., then it will make for intraday trading. However, if you buy it today at 10 a.m. and sell it tomorrow at 10 a.m., then it will not count as intraday trading. There are many advantages to intraday trading, such as lower brokerage fees, faster results, bigger profits, etc., but there is always a flipside. The risk doubles with intraday trading. The stock price might not rise as steeply as expected and, in fact, drop drastically. If this happens, there is always the choice to hold on to the stock for the long term, but if you don't have to pay for the investment, then you can take an exit on the stock with a loss. Most traders will not bother about small losses in the stock market, as both profits and losses are a part and parcel of trading. However, beginners will find it difficult to accept losses and want to experience only profits. Many beginners face a string of losses and decide to quit trading, but investing in the stock market is a tricky business and one that requires you to have a lot of patience.

If you plan on being an intraday trader, then there are many methods that you can employ to predict the future of a stock. This prediction is necessary, as you need to know when to buy a stock and when to exit it. These prediction strategies are well-crafted statistical methods that will give you near-accurate results every single time. In the next section, we will look at all these strategies in detail, and you can use them to make your own predictions.

Trend Trading

This strategy is said to be great for beginners because of the ease of its application. Trend trading is a unique strategy that helps day traders predict the rise and fall in stocks with ease. There is one rule that most day traders subscribe to – stocks that are falling in the first hour of trading will continue falling through the day, whereas stocks that are rising during the first hour of trading will continue to rise. This is a trend that is easy to predict and something that truly exists in the real world.

Thus, if a trader has stocks that are rising, then it is best to wait until it reaches its peak before vacating the position. It is also best to avoid buying the stocks that are falling. It is better to stick with predictable stocks, as opposed to those that are unpredictable. Once you get the hang of it, you will be able to predict stock fluctuations with ease.

There are a few basic rules trend traders tend to follow:
1.   Make sure that the stock has moved upwards for a while.
2.   Make sure that average over a 10-day period is greater than the monthly average.
3.   Make sure that the stock has closed at least 200 points the previous day.

Following these rules will help because these make it easier to determine which stocks are trending and when to buy and sell. This trend method allows investors to make a profit from a simple pattern, as you just have to track a stock for a few days at the most and research the stock's performance over a certain period of time.

Rebate Trading

Rebate trading is another great option for an investor. Rebate trading takes place through an electronic communication network. ECNs are where all the buying and selling take place. These ECNs require people to invest in a large number of stocks so that a market can be created. For instance, you buy 2000 stocks of company X and sell 1000 stocks of company Y. This will keep the ECN in motion, and they will pay you a certain commission for your contribution. Apart from the profit that you will make through your dealings, you will also have the chance to earn a commission from them.

ECNs are more efficient and create competition among firms. There are many advantages to this trading method. These include the lower costs, transparency, fast execution, and the fact that trading can happen after the exchange closes. This is why people prefer this type of trading.

Many consider rebate trading to be one of the safest ways of trading because of the commissions and the transparency with it since investors have – in a way – control over aspects of the market, because the markets only work if people invest.

Contrarian Trading

When it comes to the stock market, there is no one strategy that can be universally applied. It changes from person to person, and you have to adopt a strategy that you think is going to work best for you. One such reverse strategy is known as contrarian trading. A contrarian is a person who will not follow the market trend but will set his or her own path. This means that if the stock prices drop and everybody rushes to buy it, the contrarian will sell his possessions. Meanwhile, if the stock prices are rising and everybody is selling theirs to gain a profit, the contrarian will buy the stocks. This type of strategy was popularized by Warren Buffet and has become quite a popular strategy with several people, both beginners and professionals.

However, contrarian trading can both risky and safe at times. Given that people can be wrong at times, it's safe and profitable if a lot of people buy a stock that does poorly and a contrarian does not. It means that the contrarian did not lose. However, if people are correct about a stock and the contrarian did not buy, it means that the contrarian did not make a profit. While it is popular, it may not work for an investor if he or she does not have a clue on what he or she doing, but in this leap-of-faith method, the gains can outweigh the risks.

As you will see later, the contrarian trading method can be used in other markets outside of the stock market. For example, some people who invest in silver use a technique that is similar to the contrarian method as a way to control silver prices. Despite this, contrarian trading works best when it is used for stocks.

Candlestick Trading

Candlestick trading adopts a statistical method of trading. In this type of trading, a person makes use of what is known as candlesticks. Candlesticks are graphs that look like a candle, but they are just a rectangle with two lines coming out of the top and bottom half. These are statistical graphs that are used to predict the rise and fall in stocks. Say the stock price has been at a low of $30 and a high of $100; the candlestick method will allow the trader to know how the graph will shape up. He or she will use a mathematical formula that will determine where the candles need to be placed. If you are a beginner who is good in statistics, then this is the best strategy to adopt.

An interesting note about the candlestick is that it is color coded, and the colors reflect the movement of the stock. If the candle body is black or red, it means that the stock closed lower; but if it is white or green, the stock closed higher. The line between the candle body means the highest price wins on top while the low end reflects the lowest price of the day.

Price Action Trading

Just like candlesticks, there is a similar method known as price action. Here, the trader makes use of the statistics available to him or her, such as the overall price of the stock, how high it went during the day, how low it went, how it has been performing all through the week, how it has fared since its inception, etc. Everything is taken into account before any conclusion is derived. This method also makes use of a mathematical formula that you have to apply correctly to arrive at correct results.

While this approach is minimalist, price action trading is just like every other trading type. There are some advantages of using price action trading, such as being free, versatile, and works with any trading software. A disadvantage of this trading method is that someone has to be good at math, or the investor needs the time to do the mathematical formula in order to arrive at a correct conclusion. The conclusion is needed before the investor can buy or sell any stocks, which means it is time-consuming. However, it is important that anyone who wants to use this method must take the time to learn and understand this method for it to be used properly.

News Trading

News trading refers to reading news articles on a particular stock and understanding where it stands. Every day, companies release news articles on their progress, acquisitions, announcements, changes in board committee members, company forecasts, etc. All these need to be considered when you wish to invest in a company. Reading the newspaper daily or subscribing to emails from companies is a must. If you hear good news about a company, then you must quickly buy their stocks, and once everybody else reads and buys stocks, you will benefit, as the stock price will shoot up. You can then sell the stocks when they reach the day's peak.

An easier way to do news trading is to download apps that are focused on stocks and financial news if you own a smartphone. This means that the information that you need to make your stock investments is right at your fingertips, as it is common for people to have their smartphones with them. Moreover, this is a cost-efficient strategy, as many apps are either free or they cost a few dollars. This means you spend less money on either a physical or online newspaper subscription and spend less time searching your emails in order to see the news on your stocks.

This approach may seem easy compared to the others, but it's not. With news trading, you have to keep track of the dates and times of every important event. It is very important to avoid knee-jerk reactions because these could lead to higher risks and work against you if a trade goes south. However, when done correctly, news trading can be great for your portfolio.

Algorithm Trading

It is no secret that computers are far more intelligent than the human mind, so why not use their power to help with stocks and shares? One such way to employ computers to help you predict the rise and fall in the prices of stocks is known as algorithm trading. Algorithm trading is a method where computer software helps you arrive at a prediction graph for a stock. All you need to do is feed in information about the stock, and it will take care of the rest. However, you need to update it regularly in order to have a consistent supply of information. One thing to remember is that the computer will not be 100% accurate and will only predict the most likely consequence.

That being said, if you are planning to, or already work for an institution that buys shares in large amounts daily, then algorithm trading is your best bet. This is because algorithm trading is perfect for keeping track of a large amount of stocks, as a computer can look at more things in a shorter amount of time. Moreover, this is great for those who do not have time to figure stock placement but need information in a short amount of time.

Fundamental Trading

Fundamental trading refers to checking the fundamentals of a company. This means that the balance sheet and other vital information of the company must be checked before making an investment. If everything looks good, then it is a good stock to invest in. However, if the company has a lot of debts and has not been doing too well of late, then it is best to avoid buying its shares. Many people don't think it is important to check fundamentals when indulging in day trading, but they fail to understand that once you buy and sell the stocks of a company, you will want to continue doing it for the coming weeks or until such time as you feel you have made enough use of the company's fluctuating stock prices. So in this regard, you must check its fundamentals.

This type of trading is great for those who checked everything about a company before investing, as those who did will most likely avoid falling for any hype risks. If you correctly find any current stock position and the prices that go along with it, then you are likely to be successful and make money from trades.

Sentiment Trading

Just like checking the fundamentals of the company, you need to check how people are viewing the company. You need to have an understanding of the market's mood and how people perceive the company. There is a combination of contrarians and fundamentalists in the market, and you have to assess which comprises the majority. Once you find out, you can invest in a company based on your style of trading. An experienced trader will not take too long to assess the mood towards a company.

As the name suggests, this type of trading is based on emotions. Unlike candlestick and algorithm trading, there are no mathematical equations, only what you feel. The best way to make money from this is to find stocks that the market considers either overvalued or undervalued. Then, figure out which to buy and trade. Sentiment trading is risky if you are wrong because you are not looking for a short-term profit, as attitudes about trades can change rapidly at times.

Pattern Trading

Pattern trading refers to looking at the pattern of the stock and how it has been behaving. For this, you need to observe its trend for at least a month or two. You have to see its graph and know exactly when it dips during the month and when it rises. Once you have all these mapped out, you will know when the stock price will rise and when it will fall. Establishing a pattern is always a good idea, as relying on trustworthy information is always a boon in the stock market.

The best rule for pattern trading is that you should be careful with margins or borrowed funds, as losses can happen quickly if you do not know what you are doing. Moreover, it is possible for someone to lose the initial investment and more, so it is important to know whether your information is trustworthy or not.

Pivot Trading

Pivot trading is used to know how high a stock will go and how low it will fall. This is important for an intraday trader to assess, as he or she has to buy stock when it reaches its lowest and sell it when it reaches its highest. Buying just before it reaches its high is a poor strategy that a rookie may end up doing. It is important for a trader to know when the best time is to buy the stocks and trigger off a buy call on the price. Similarly, he or she will have to trigger off a sell call and make the most of the stock's price fluctuations.

For those wondering, the definition of a pivot point would be calculated by averaging the prior day's closing prices, both lows and highs. This method is very mathematical, as analysis is usually done using a series of calculations to identify a stock's resistance and support levels. This calculation is used as a reactionary price level, which helps people indicate how the stock will fare in the market. Pivot trading can work for any market, but it is perfect for those who want to trade in markets, such as the spot currency market.

Fading

Fading is a strategy that is good for contrarians. If some people end up buying a stock owing to some good news, then the fader will quickly sell it off, as the price of the share will drop because of over buying. Fading is an important strategy to adopt and one that will help you get rid of useless stocks from your portfolio. It's great for short-term gains, but the strategy itself is volatile.

An example of fading would be a contrarian selling a stock in high demand for one that has a low ratio between price and earning. Let's say a contrarian sells a stock from a social media IPO, such as Facebook, for a stock like eBay. In this situation, the contrarian saves money, as the price of the Facebook stock will go down because everyone is buying. If the eBay stock were to go up, then the contrarian will start fading again.

Type of Stocks to Look for

When it comes to choosing your stocks, there are a few things that you need to consider, as explained below.

Type

The first thing to consider is the type of stocks to buy. There are two types of stocks available, namely, preference stock and common stock. Preference stocks are only available to the top-level employees of the company or to employees in general. These stocks are said to have more value, as they are firsthand stocks and not yet traded on the share market. As stated in the previous chapter, these are IPOs or initial public offerings, which is a good scheme for beginners to take up. They may purchase the stocks at a discounted price, and this will ensure that the stocks will fetch a better price when sold in the market. However, if the share is not doing so well in the market, then holding on to it is pretty much useless. Conversely, if the stock is doing well, then selling it in the secondary market is a good option. You will also be eligible for a set rate of interest regularly on preference stocks.

Common stocks are equity stocks that are traded in the market. These are secondary stocks. Owning these can be quite beneficial, as the company will consider these before preference shares to repay any investment in case of a company wind up. Common stocks, however, will not give you a set rate of interest and will fluctuate based on the company's progress.

Preference stock differs from common stock in another important way, as common stockholders can be shareholders while preference stockholders have no voting rights in the company.

For those looking for examples of the two stock types, here is one. An example of a company offering preferred stock is Bank of America while social media giant Twitter offers common stock. This means that people with stock in Bank of America will not have a company voting right, but they will get their dividend first. Meanwhile, Twitter stockholders have a voting right, but they are last in getting a dividend.

News

Have an eye on the news at all times. You must know when a company declares profits or results and how these will impact the stocks. Buy stock that will rise in value every time the company declares profits. This will ensure that you make some profit while also having the chance to sell the stock when the face value rises. You can subscribe to news emails and buy a newspaper that gives you information on companies and their results. These results are declared every three months and are known as quarterly results. Depending on the type of results that are declared, you can buy stocks of the company.

As mentioned previously, for those who want instant access to news, there are apps for you to download to keep track of stocks. Apple automatically puts a stock app on their devices, so iPhone users don't necessarily have to download any apps, but it is better that they do. Many people find the default stock app terrible, but that is up to the iPhone user to decide. Android users, unlike iPhone users, do not have a default stock app. No matter what type of smartphone you use, you can find apps in both the Google and Apple app stores. Some stock apps are free, while others cost money, but read the reviews before downloading to see if the app meets your financial news needs.

Profits/Losses

Profits play an important role when it comes to choosing stocks. It is obvious that you will want the stocks of a company that declares good profits and helps you build a wealthy empire. However, if a company randomly throws up a loss, then you must not abandon it. Both profits and losses are part of a company's results, and you cannot expect only profits. However, if you think that the company is consistently declaring losses and refusing to pay any dividends to its shareholders, then it is best to do away with shares belonging to that company. Sometimes, the results of the company don't impact its share price. In such a case, you can trade with it on an intraday basis.

There are people who believe that not conducting research on the profit and loss history of a company can lead people into making bad investment decisions, as they do not know if the company is consistently performing poorly. In fact, these same people claim that it is one of the most common reasons why people lose money in stocks. Avoid making a bad investment by either researching it yourself or by having a broker help you understand whether a company is a good investment or not.

Fundamentals

The fundamentals of the company are always important. You need to read all its profit and loss statements to get a good idea of where a company stands. If you think the company is good enough, then there should be nothing stopping you from buying their stocks. However, if you think they have a lot of unpaid debts, then it is best to steer clear of this company. Don't take any company for granted, as even the big ones will borrow money from time to time to fund their projects. If they fail to repay these loans, then their balance sheet will look bad.

It is always important to research a company's fundamentals before investing. You need to know where the company stands, so it is important to research such aspects of a company as cash flow, asset returns, shareholder earning and returns, and retention of future growth. These aspects will give you an idea of where the company is going. However, it does not mean you will turn a profit with a company that has good fundamentals because you never know what can happen in the markets.

Recommendations

If someone recommends good shares to you, then you can buy some, but you must do your research as well. If you don't do your homework, then you alone will suffer the consequences. It is also important to know who to take advice from and who not to trust. Don't trust everything you read on the Internet, as it can be full of spurious and dubious recommendations. Although your broker will also ask you to buy certain stocks, it is best that you do your own research to avoid falling prey to bad stock recommendations.

Failure to do research can lead to a loss. Recommendations are a perfect example of why you should always do your own research. Always be suspicious of any deal that sounds too good to be true. As anyone can give bad advice, it is important for you to minimize your risks. Research can help you avoid making any bad investments.

Availability

When you wish to buy the stocks of a company, make sure you look at the number of buyers and sellers for it. If your share call is stuck with millions of others, then you may never get your stocks on time or at the price of your choice. So make sure you look at the figures to determine whether or not your stocks will be approved. The same goes for selling the stock. If you are in line with millions of others, then the chances of your stocks getting absorbed might be low. So you need to strategize and wait it out, or sell the stocks before they go into freezing or lock down.

It is important to understand why stocks have availability. Availability helps prevents stocks from running out, and it keeps demand in control. While it is inconvenient for you, it keeps the amount of stocks and their demand in control. This means that you have work on your timing to buy or sell your stocks. This skill will also help you with making profits and building your portfolio.

Allocating

You must allocate your portfolio investments in such a way that you have a few long-term stocks, along with some short-term and some medium-term stocks. All of these are important, and you cannot forgo some of them and concentrate on just one type. Allocate them in such way that not more than 8% to 10% of your total investment is placed into one stock. If you go overboard and buy a lot of stocks of the same company, then you will be increasing your risk instead of diversifying it, as allocating tries to balance your risk and rewards.

With allocating, there is no set formula, as everyone, and every portfolio, is different. However, it is recommended that you hold on to stocks for at least five years. In mutual funds, a target date might be added as a way to provide an investor's portfolio-based solution that is dependent on his or her individual situation by looking at such factors as risk appetite, age, etc. Although many think that target date is problematic, it can be useful to some, as it can help balance risk and reward.

Stop Loss Shares

You must always use the stop loss method when you pick shares. This is mainly for intraday traders, as it is important not to lose any money on your investment. If you don't have a stop loss in place, then you will end up not selling your stocks on the very same day. You will be tempted to hold on to them and not have the chance to sell them in the near future. This is why having a stop loss can be beneficial to everyone, as it can limit investor loss.

The advantage of stop loss is that it doesn't cost you anything to place a stop loss order. Moreover, you don't have to monitor your investment on a daily basis if you don't want to, and it keeps you from making emotional decisions as it cuts your losses for you. However, a disadvantage of stop loss is that it can be activated by a short-term change in price stock, so you have to be careful picking the stop loss percentage.

There are no set rules on how stop loss should be placed, as that depends on your investing style. Stop loss is a great tool to use that many people ignore, but keep in mind that this tool may not make a profit for you.

Swinging Shares

Swinging is a technique in which day traders indulge in combined stop loss and fresh position trading. This means that they choose a stop loss, and if they do exist there, they reassume a fresh position from the same spot. The general belief is that, if a stock does go down, then it is bound to go up again. Thus, by assuming a fresh position, the trader will get the stock at a good price and then sell it when it goes up. This means that day traders have to keep the stock at least overnight to make sure that they are getting a fresh position.

A great way to use swinging is to look at patterns (like using the candlestick method in reverse) as a way to see if you can make a profit.

Special Shares

Special shares are those that are issued to shareholders who are already holding a few shares of the company. These special shares will not be available to everyone and will be issued to loyal holders who have been holding shares for a long time. These may be in the form of bonus shares or just initial public offerings that are opened to existing shareholders of a company. These special shares are always a good investment and are sure to help you diversify your portfolio.

Another advantage of special shares that people get is the fact that some companies give these shareholders more voting rights in the company. This means that these shareholders can become involved in making important decisions in that company. It also helps against hostile takeovers. Although hostile takeovers are rare, people who received more voting rights through special shares can stop hostile takeovers from succeeding.

Insurance Shares

Insurance stock is a very special case. When you think of insurance, you don't think of a company in the stock markets. However, you can invest in insurance companies themselves in the stock market. Many insurance companies are in the marketplace; it doesn't matter what kind of insurance the company sells. Companies from which you can purchase stock include MetLife, Aflac, and Progressive. However, not all insurance shares belong to common stocks.

There are two different types of insurance stocks. Public companies like MetLife, Aflac, and Progressive are members of the stock exchange. You can buy and sell these stocks whenever you want, although they are considered to be long-term investments. You should only do so if you feel like that you're not seeing a return after a few years.

The other type of insurance share is a mutual company. This type of company is owned by the policyholder and is a fund. You will learn more about funds in the next chapter.

What are Options?

Options are a type of security that are high risk yet pay excessive profits if done right. Unlike stocks and bonds, options are not paid in full from the get go. That is, you have the option to reserve something and then decide on whether you wish to buy it or leave it. That "choice to buy or leave" is your "option." Let us look at an example for you to understand it better.

Let us say you wish to buy a nice air conditioner for your home. The owner is giving it at a nominal value of $200. However, you don't have that much with you, so you ask the seller to reserve it for you for one month and then pay him $50 in advance for it. He will agree and reserve it for you for a month. Now, halfway through, you find out that the air conditioner was previously owned by Johnny Depp, and so, its value now stands at $500. Now, given that the seller has agreed to sell it for $200 to you, he is obligated to not raise the price for it. Once you get the AC, you need to pay the balance of $150, and you can then sell it at $500 to make a profit of $300. However, if halfway through, you find out that the seller has cheated you because the AC is not in working condition, and repairing it would cost you $100, then it is best that you do not buy it at all, but you will have to lose your $50, which you paid in advance. This is good, as at least you didn't have to pay the $150, which would have been a bigger loss. If you forget to pay before the expiry date, then you will lose the deal.

Similarly, consider the stocks as the air conditioner here, and the deal as your option.

In the stock market, you can reserve securities that you think are worth it and then wait on them. These underlying securities can be stocks, bonds, gold, foreign currencies, future securities, etc. If they are really rising in value, then buy at your agreed rate, and then sell them when they are high. If they are going down, then don't buy them at all.

Once you get the hang of it, you will know which ones to reserve and which ones not to.

Alan Anderson

When the person is waiting for the price to go up and has reserved a stock, then it is called a "call" option, and when a person is trying to sell within a specified time and is waiting for the price to drop, then it's called a "put" option.

Advantages of Investing in Options

The advantage of investing in options is that you have a chance to get good stocks at a nominal value and can wait on them to grow in value before paying for them in full. So a stock worth $1000 can be bought for $100, and you can wait for it to go to $2000 before buying it. In case it doesn't, then you will only lose $100 and not $1000. Thus, there is high risk but also high reward with this type of investment. It depends on the type of option that you choose for yourself. It is fine to make a few errors at the very beginning, as it may be seen as a learning curve, but you must take notes and make wise investment choices for yourself.

Other advantages include cost, potential returns, and flexibility. If done correctly, a person can use options to mimic a stock position for a lower price and make a profit, thus leading to a higher return. Options are very flexible, and they can work with any type of trading method. At times, options are less risky than stocks because they require less commitment than stocks. Moreover, there are options that protect stock positions and stop losses at a certain point.

Disadvantages of Investing in Options

The disadvantage is that stock prices do not fluctuate so drastically. Similar to how you will not come across items pre-owned by movie stars every day, you will not come across big stocks at low prices that will drastically go up within a week or two. Thus, if speculating is not your forte, then it is best that you not take up options at all.

Remember that options investments are risk capital investments. This means that the capital you invest in your options is quite risky, as it can go either way for you. You might get a lot of money out of it or get only little from it. In either case, you will have to be fully prepared to handle the consequences. It might sound daunting, but don't think that options are a safe bet for you as a beginner, as it is anything but that!

It is also good to remember that options have expiration dates, and if you do not sell or trade them before or on that date, they become worthless. Moreover, it is quite easy to lose money in options in other ways, such as by being wrong about the price direction of stocks. As stated above, this investment is very risky. It may not work out for you, but if it does, then it was worth the risk.

Types of Options

When it comes to options, there are certain types based on their time and expiry dates. Four types are explained below.

American Options

An American option is the most used form of option in the market today. This type of scheme allows you to exercise your right of sale anytime between the sale date and the expiration date. Say you bought a call for company X in December 2014, and its expiry date is December 2015. Now, you have the chance to sell it at any point in time and not have to wait for its expiry date. If you think you will get a lucrative deal out of it in March 2015, then you can sell it at that point in time. This type of option is great for those investing a large sum of money in options. It is hassle-free and will allow you to buy and sell your options whenever you wish to. If you think you have sold it short, you can always buy it back and sell it during its next expiry. Keeping such a motion going will help you remain invested and also book profits every now and then.

Other important information about American options is when you want to exercise your options. On a weekly setting, the last day to do this is on the Friday in the week that the option contract expires. For monthly, the last day is the third Friday of every month.

Here, the term "American" does not signify the options' limit to be exercised in America alone. The term has no geographic relevance whatsoever. However, if you are wondering why the term uses the word "American," this is because the majority of the options are from America-based companies.

European Options

The other type of option is known as European options. European options are not as flexible as American options. Here, you only have the chance to sell your options at the time of expiry. So say you bought a call for company Y in July 2015, and its expiry is July 2016. You can only sell it in July 2016, which is the expiry date of the option. So even if you were to get a great deal in February 2016 when the prices of the stocks would have reached an all-time high, you will not be able to sell your options. This type of trading is not employed because of the high amount of risk that it brings along with it. However, the option is always available to you, and you can choose it if you don't mind selling a stock close to its expiry date.

Remember the OTC (over-the-counter) markets mentioned earlier? Well, this is where the European options are normally traded. This is another reason why this option is risky, because OTC markets have fewer regulations than the standard exchanges.

Again, the name has no geographic relevance and does not pertain to options carried out in Europe alone. It can be practiced anywhere in the world.

Short-Term Options

Short-term options are those that have a short expiry period. This can vary between weeks to a month, but it depends on the country. In general, it is almost like intraday trading, where the time period is set as one day or one week. Given that this is a short-term option, it will be within a two-week period to a month's time. Rarely will it extend beyond that. This type of option is great for beginners, who will have the chance to capitalize on their investment within a short amount of time and not have to wait for a long time before seeing any results. However, the disadvantage is that the stock prices will not drastically rise and fall, such that the investor might not get a lot of money on his or her investment. In case there is a loss, there might not be much time left to recover, and the investor will have to settle for a loss. Thus, short-term options can prove to be both a boon and a bane. The best thing to do is to look for short-term options that appear quite lucrative. If you invest in them, then you can sell them at any time before the expiry date and come into a profit.

However, to make the most out of short-term options, you must understand some basic concepts. You need to watch any optional stocks you want to invest in by looking at patterns, the market trends concerning the stock, and its moving averages. You will also have to read the technical analysis on the stock and look for any indicators to buy and sell it. It is also important to try and control any risks by setting any stops within 10% to 15% of the price you bought it at.

Long-Term Options

Long-term options, unlike short-term options, are held for a long time. This means that they are not limited to just two weeks or a month and can be held for a year or more. Generally, any option that is held for a year is known as a long-term option. Thus, if you were to buy a call option on 31st March 2015, and its expiry lies on 31st March 2016, then it will count as a long-term option. Long-term options are a good choice, as you have a bigger sale window and can capitalize on the stock's highest value. Even if it has dipped in between, you have the chance to wait for its price to rise again. This exposure to price changes is a good opportunity for first-time investors to study the market. These are better known as Long Term Equity Anticipation Securities or LEAPS. These options are available not only for your regular stocks alone, but also for future securities like Amex. Some people think the extra time that they get to decide whether they keep or sell the stock makes it a bit confusing and, thus, steer clear from these types of options.

However, the term itself is very subjective. For example, a buy-and-hold investor would think that having an option less than a couple of years would be a short-term investment. Meanwhile, a day trader would consider holding an option for the same period, as the buy-and-hold investor is a long-term investment. It is important to know how long you want the stock and when to trade.

Exotic Options

Exotic options are those that are not your standard or regular options. Anything that is not regular is an exotic option. These options come with special and different privileges. These types are not too common and are only chosen by high-end investors. These also come with their fair share of gains and losses. Some of the exotic options include Asian options, digital options, barrier options, etc.

These are the different choices of options that you can choose from for your investments. You can either opt for just one of these or have a combined portfolio. However, it is always a good choice to consult an expert for some advice, as there can be some problems like pricing issues and other risks associated with the OTC, as many of the exotic options are traded in OTC. Although there are many risks, some of these risks can work for an investor.

Example of an Option Call

Let us look at two examples to see what call and put options are all about.

Let's say you buy a call option of company X for $50 a share. You pay an advance of $100 for it and buy 100 shares of the company. You then wish to pay the rest in two weeks' time. You know that the company is about to declare its results and that it will affect the stock price. You wish to wait for a week and take a call on it after the company declares the results. Say in a weeks' time, your risk pays off, and the company declares great results. The per-share value has now gone up to $60. You will now have the chance to buy the 100 shares at $50 rather than the revised price of $60.

You will have a profit of $900. Now, you may wonder as to why you earn $900 out of it. Well, you paid $50 for each share, and after the revision, the value went up to $60. That leaves you with a profit of $1000 from it, but you already paid $100 for it, which will have to be deducted from your profits. That leaves you with a profit of $900 on your investment.

Here, you will wonder why this is any different from buying the stock in the first place, and that is a good question. The advantage of this deal is that the person has the chance to increase the rate of interest on this deal as opposed to buying the stock. Thus, investing in options is always a good choice.

You won't have to pay in full either way.

Now let's look at a reverse scenario. Suppose you bought the stock by paying the $100 and expected the share price to rise. However, once the results were announced, the price of the stock dropped. This means that you will be overpaying for a low-value stock. So it is your right to cancel the deal or wait for it to expire.

A buyer's call is known as the buyer's right to buy the call from the seller at a fixed price or set a future price for it. This call is important as the price of the stock might decline in the coming days. The buyer's call will ensure that the buyer does not overpay for the stock. The seller, however, will be hoping for the price to decline, as he will benefit.

A seller's call is the opposite of a buyer's call. Here, the seller has the right to set the price of the stock on a future date. This is an advantage for the seller, as the price might rise. So selling it to the buyer at a lower rate will cost the seller and cause a loss.

Commodities Trade

Commodities trade refers to trading commodities in the market on a regular basis. These commodities are nothing but everyday commodities that you use in your day-to-day life. Commodities have traded in the market since time immemorial. They are traded to keep their prices consistent in the market and to enable investors to have a return on their investment. The commodities market is quite volatile, and the prices will not remain constant for long. There are many types of commodities that are traded in the market, and each one commands a different price.

When you trade in commodities, it is known as future trading. This is because you are fixing a future price for it and buying and selling it to realize a profit. Just like options, there will be an expiry date for these, within which time you must sell your possession. You will be required to pay for it if you don't quit your position by the end of the day.

There are four main categories of commodities trade, and they are given below.

Metals

This is probably the most traded of all commodities. Metals refer to everyday metals, such as nickel, iron, copper, etc., which are used in both industries and other non-industrial businesses. Metal prices rise and fall based on the demand for them. Apart from these, precious metals like gold, silver, and platinum are also traded in the market. These metals are an important part of many industries, and the demand for them will never deplete. You can choose any one of the metals and keep a close watch on their prices for a month before you decide to invest in them.

There are some advantages of investing in metals. The first is that it is on a global scale, as every country in the world uses metals in some capacity. This investment can also make your portfolio diverse, because people tend to invest in stocks and funds more. The main disadvantage is the price to get into investing metals, as it is more expensive. Even the everyday metals, not just precious metals, are somewhat expensive to buy. However, it might be worth looking into, as there is a global demand for it.

While we go into more details about precious metals in Chapter 4, there are multiple ways to trade them. You can buy stocks, mutual funds, options, and ETFs (which will be explained in Chapter 4). Like commodities, all of these investments are very risky and always in demand because of their everyday and industrial uses.

Livestock

The next type of commodity that is traded on the market is known as livestock. As the name suggests, livestock refers to live animals and also meat. Meat, such as pork, lamb, and chicken, are traded. Many factors determine their price. These factors include weather conditions, breeding conditions, etc. You must keep an eye on the news to see what is impacting livestock. You can also trade in live animals, such as pigs, sheep, and horses. Don't worry as you don't have to buy these or shelter them; you are only dealing in their prices and are interested in their fluctuations alone.

An advantage of investing in livestock is that it can grow the economy, as job growth can happen because of farms needing more help with livestock. However, there are disadvantages to this investment related to such issues as air and water pollution and global warming. However, this investment is useful anywhere, as many countries use livestock.

Agriculture

Agricultural produce is the next type of commodity traded in the market. Agricultural produce, such as sugar, rice, wheat, barley, potatoes, onions, corn, etc., are all traded in the commodities market. Their prices will fluctuate, and you will have the chance to capitalize on these fluctuations. As you know, many factors will determine the ultimate price. These factors include weather, rain, heat, pests, government policies, farmer strikes, etc., all of which will ultimately determine whether the price of the commodity will rise or plummet. This type of commodity is slightly more predictable than others, so this maybe a good entry point for you in the commodities trade market.

Just like livestock, the advantage of an agriculture investment is that job growth can happen, as farms will need more people to help out with producing commodities, thus leading to a bigger return for investors. The main disadvantage is water shortages, given that agriculture needs water. However, if there is a drought, this will lead to less production. If you want to invest in this market, it is important to research it before going in, as it is risky although more reliable than the other commodity markets.

Energy

Energies, such as oil and gas, are traded in the commodities market. Energy resources are needed on a daily basis, and their prices will obviously fluctuate. It is important that you understand how important it is for you to read the news and understand the various factors that affect the prices of energy resources. Once you understand the pattern, you will have the chance to predict the price difference.

The main advantage of energy investment is that many energy investments are UITs (unit investment trusts). UITs have a tax exemption status in the U.S., so American investors have a way to deduct this investment on their yearly tax returns. However, there are many disadvantages in this market. For example, there may be production fees involved, such as paying for pumping oil or replacement parts for the equipment used in production. It is also extremely risky, as gas and oil production can stop for any reason, such as the supply depletion.

If you want that tax exemption status, talk to a broker to see if the energy investment qualifies.

These form the various categories of commodities that are traded, and you can choose one or more of these depending on how much money you have at your disposal.

When it comes to commodity trading, there are many things you must bear in mind, and they are given below.

First, you must agree to deal in the commodity without having a chance to touch and feel whatever you are buying. It is not possible for you to touch and buy the sugar and the rice, and you will have to settle for whatever quality is up for trade. Many times, the quality will not match your expectations and might end up being much lower. However, given that you will not take possession of it, you must not really be bothered about it.

You will have to make a minimum investment when you wish to deal in commodities. You cannot enter a commodity market with just a small monetary margin. The risk factor is quite high, and you must invest enough to cut your losses and walk away with a profit. If you invest a little and gain out of it, then well and good, but if you invest a little and lose all of it, then it will be useless.

Hedging is a prevalent practice in the commodities market. Hedging refers to buying a commodity at the current price and then deciding on selling it at a set price. That way, you will avoid the need to face any price fluctuation problems, and your return on investment will be guaranteed. This can be seen as a safe option, but one that is a good choice for those interested in safeguarding their investments.

You must understand that these commodity prices will fluctuate for the same reasons behind stock value fluctuations. Thus, if there is an excess demand for a commodity, then its price will rise. If there is no demand for it, then the prices will fall. Now, say for example winter is approaching, and the demand for sheep's wool has gone up. The price for sheep will consistently rise until winter has passed and then rapidly fall. Thus, trading sheep in summer is not such a good idea.

One important consideration to make is that, unlike the stock market where the values will somehow manage to return to normalcy even if the company is not faring too well, several factors, such as manmade disasters and natural calamities, can cause the commodities market to come to a halt. Thus, if you have made a big investment and the expiry date is near, but a natural calamity has taken place, then the chances are that your investment will go bad. So it is not advisable to wait until the very end to execute a deal, and you must do away with it as soon as possible.

An example of a natural calamity affecting investments would be a drought if you had an agricultural investment. Let's say that you invested in a farm in a state that rarely suffers from a drought. However, near the expiration date of your investment, the state had a very dry year. This would mean that your investment became useless because nature worked against you, which caused you to lose money.

You should be ready to understand the global impact on these commodities, as their prices will be influenced by many global economic factors. It is not limited to local factors, as so many other ones will come into play. Thus, the prices in your country can be affected by the political and economic conditions in another country. There is always a certain amount of risk associated with these commodities, but you will have the chance to expose your portfolio to global markets.

These form the various ideals that you must keep in mind when you wish to trade in the commodities market. Remember, you must do your own research before entering a market, and make sure that you have enough knowledge and also a fair idea of the risks involved before you decide to make an investment.

Chapter 3: Investing In Bonds And Mutual Funds

In the previous chapter, we looked at stocks and options and how each one operates. We now shift our focus to bonds and mutual funds and look at how they function.

What are Bonds?

It is no secret that you need a lot of capital to start a business. You cannot break into your piggy bank and decide to start a Fortune 500 company. You will need lots of money to flow in, which you can utilize to set up your business. Now, not all companies will have the capacity to apply for bank loans and try and fund their business. They will need help from investors, who will invest in the company to help it grow. This is why companies decide to issue bonds, which common people buy, and the money they use to buy these bonds is what finances the company.

So if a company issues you a bond, it will be much less than the face value of the bond. They will promise to pay you back the full amount in, say, five years' time and, in the meantime, pay you a 10% profit on a yearly basis. This means that not only will you get your money back in the end, but you will also get a 10% monthly/yearly profit from it.

In order for you to buy a bond, you need to be confident about the company and whether it will progress well over a period of time. If you are buying the bonds of an already established company that is looking to raise funds for a new project, then the risk might be lower. However, if you are for investing in a new company, then it is best to exercise caution and do your research.

Advantages of Investing in Bonds

The advantage of investing in bonds is that you will have your money safe, and the rate of interest agreed upon will be paid out on a yearly basis. You need not worry about losing your money or wasting it on unnecessary things. You will have the option of buying the bonds directly by asking your broker to buy them for you, or you can invest in them by way of mutual funds. We will learn about these in the next section.

Moreover, bonds, especially those that are either short-term or medium term, have lower volatility than stocks, making bonds safer investments. While it is safer, it does not mean that there are no risks involved; it is not risk-free. However, there is some legal protection for bondholders, as they will receive some money in the event that the company becomes bankrupt.

Disadvantages of Investing in Bonds

The disadvantage of investing in bonds is that the rate being promised might not be good enough, and the person might get a better return on investment by choosing to save the principal amount in a bank. Another disadvantage is that the principal amount might not get paid back if the company is facing severe losses. If you have chosen the option to get your money back at any time before the maturity, then you can save your money; if not, you might have to deal with losses.

One of the biggest disadvantages is that the bond issuer's credit rating might affect the bond prices, which can make the bond volatile. For example, if the issuer's credit rating goes down unexpectedly, then your bond's market price will go down. If the market price goes down, it may affect the selling price. For example, if this happens and you decide to sell once it hits maturity, then you will have a lower selling price. This can affect your profit from the sale, and it's a risk that might happen with bonds.

Government Bonds

Government bonds are those that are issued by the government. This means that these bonds are securities that the government of your country will issue to you. Government bonds can be issued by both the central and the state government. These bonds are money that the government borrows from the public. The government needs this money to carry out their various businesses, including construction, renovation, repair, etc. Although the government will already have some money, it cannot operate on that money alone.

These types of bonds have existed for a long time, and the government has issued millions of bonds to date. That makes for a debt of nearly 20 trillion dollars owing to all the bonds that have been issued to date. Here, you must understand that the government will collect taxes from citizens and try to recover the money for the bonds. However, the amount collected will often be insufficient, and several bonds would have reached maturity date. Now, they cannot turn away the people that they have not paid as yet, and they must ensure that everybody gets their money. Under such a circumstance, they will borrow this money and pay off their bondholders. Doing this for a long time can cause the economy of a country to destabilize. This destabilization can affect those who invest in stocks as people are not going to spend as much during an economic crisis, no matter how big or small it is seems.

However, from an investor's point of view, this is a good investment, as there is very little credit risk at play. This means that there is no real danger of the investor not getting his or her money back in full. Thus, government bonds make for a good choice for all those looking for a safe option to invest in.

However, you must remember that your credit risk needs to be high if you wish to make the most of your investment. "High risk, high reward" is the ultimate anthem of the stock market, and with bonds, that is not a possibility. Although there will be the danger of you losing half or all your money in credit risk investments, the possibility of doubling or even tripling is high. This makes it a worthwhile investment for you because you don't have to worry about suffering any losses.

There are different types of government bonds that you can choose from. Each one comes with its own set of advantages, and you have to choose the one that suits your investment type the best. Many brokers these days will advise you against investing in these bonds, as the American debt level is consistently rising. However, the ultimate choice lies with you alone, and you will have to decide for yourself whether you want to invest in government bonds.

The type of bond you can buy from the government is dependent on the bond's maturity. Short-term bonds are called bills, and they mature in less than a year. Notes are medium-term bonds that mature between one and 10 years. Meanwhile, bonds themselves are the long-term ones that take more than 10 years to mature.

These bonds are better known as treasury bonds or treasury bills.

There are some advantages of investing in treasury bonds. These bring great diversity to your portfolio, and these types of bonds can be bought and sold in the common markets. However, a great disadvantage of these bonds is the rarity of a fiscal crisis within the government, as people will start to wonder if their bond will be honored.

Agency Bonds

Agency bonds, like government bonds, are issued by companies that are sponsored by the government. These agencies are not run, but are taken care of, by the government. They are financed and looked after by the federal government, and so, they can be considered as being just as trustworthy as the government. Many of these companies are finance-based. An example of a company that offers agency bonds is Sallie Mae.

There are several types of agencies, such as the USAID and Small Business Administration, which are affiliated with the federal government. They are set up to run parallel businesses for the government and will thus require separate funding.

This funding is collected from the public by issuing bonds. These bonds will follow the same route mapped out by the government bonds. There will be a date of issuance and a date of expiry. Once the bond expires, the person will get back the principal sum, along with an attached rate of interest. However, these bonds will not provide the same guarantee as your regular government bonds, so there is always the risk of bad credit that will loom over these bonds. You must be prepared to accept whatever is given to you.

One major disadvantage of these bonds is that they will create a hassle if you try to buy them in bulk. Thus, trying to buy large volumes of these bonds by paying large sums of money will set you back a few weeks' time. This is unlike regular government bonds, which will be issued within the same day or within a matter of minutes. Therefore, all those trying to buy these in bulk had better consider government bonds as opposed to these bonds.

Another disadvantage has to do with the issues with taxes that these bonds can cause. Some agency bonds are taxable at the federal, state, and local levels, whereas others are only taxed by the federal government. It is important to research not only whether your agency bond is taxable, but also to whom you have to pay the taxes, whether it be the federal government, your state, or your local government.

One positive thing here is that these bonds will pay you a rate of interest that is better than that of regular government bonds or treasuries. This means that they make for a better option if you don't mind handling a little risk and expect a higher yield from your investment. Don't worry about the loss, as that is quite rare. Most of these agencies deliver on their promise.

Besides, having government backing will still be better than having no proper backing. You will realize that these are a safer bet than the other forms of bonds.

Municipal Bonds

As previously mentioned, apart from the federal government, state and local governments also issue bonds to their citizens. These governments will need money for the upkeep of the city. It is important to realize that these will not pay an interest rate as high as the federal government would, but the rate will nevertheless be good.

Municipal bonds, like regular government bonds, are free of risk, as they are backed by the government. They will not carry a high credit risk, and so, their payback will also not be too high. However, you can look to them, as they will provide you with security.

At this time, around 1.5 million bonds have been issued in total. This means that their trade is still pretty rampant. There are times when the government will not have any project at hand. During such times, the government will not be able to issue any bonds to the public. However, they will issue a promissory note, which will state that the bond will be approved once a project is envisaged.

There are three types of mutual bonds for you to choose. There is a general obligation (GO) bond, which is the most secure because it has a low interest rate. The revenue of the bond is made from a specified source, such as an incoming project. The last bond is an assessment bond, which is a bond that is repaid from collected taxes.

One of the main advantages of this bond is that it has a lower risk factor when compared to stocks. It is also worth a lot in the secondary market, and there is a chance for income growth. However, there are some disadvantages as well. It costs more to start a municipal bond, as a bigger payoff is dependent on how much money you spent to start off with. Another risk is defaulting, which can lead to a loss of capital. Defaulting is very rare, but it can happen if everything that could go wrong happens. However, it is important that you do research to make sure that municipal bonds are for you.

These, just like government bonds, are free of tax and will not eat away into your profits.

Corporate Bonds

Corporate bonds are issued by corporations, such as big businesses and multinational companies. Corporate bonds are issued by these companies to people interested in funding their business. This is like a return on investment from a business venture.

Corporate bonds are used by companies to raise capital for several reasons. Some of these include raising money to pay for shareholders' dividends or cutting down on any losses that the company might have suffered to have enough operating capital at any given point.

Whatever the reason, they will borrow money from people and issue them bonds. The rate of interest that they pay will always be much higher than what governments pay. Thus, you will get a higher rate of interest on your investment in these bonds. In fact, the rate of interest is generally double or even triple as compared to your regular government, agency, or municipal bonds.

There are many advantages of investing in corporate bonds. There are strong returns on your investment, and they have liquidity, which means that in the secondary markets, you can make a profit when you sell when the prices rise and buy when prices drop. Another advantage is offered by the three bond options, namely, short-term, medium-term, or long-term.

However, there are several disadvantages associated with these types of bonds. It is obvious that a lot of credit risk will be attached, owing to the high rate of interest that these bonds provide. You might get your money back in full or lose your money, if it comes to that. You can also lose money when there is an event risk, which is an event in which a company has issues with money, such as cash flow. It's important to remember that interest and principal payments are dependent on a company's cash flow.

There is something known as junk bonds that you can purchase for yourself. These bonds are high-risk and high-reward bonds that will pay you back a lot more than you would expect a government bond to pay you. Thus, you have the chance to increase your return on investment by choosing this type of bond.

Zero Coupon Bonds

Zero coupon bonds are basic bonds that follow extremely simple rules. Here, there are no complications, and everything is straightforward. Now, say for example you buy bonds worth $400 today that have an expiry date five years from now. Once

Alan Anderson

they reach their maturity period, these bonds will be worth $800 each. So for a period of five years, you will receive a consistent rate of interest for your investment. These are extremely safe choices for you, and the rate of interest is also higher than what your federal government or agency would pay.

Here, the bond that you receive today will actually be worth $800. However, you will get it at a big discount now and then cash it in, in full, after a certain amount of time. Don't think of this as a bad scheme, as your money will be safe, and you will have the chance to double what you have in due course.

It is, however, not comparable to stocks, as it might not take so long to receive a return on your investment. Bonds are safer options for you, but you will not be able to invite large returns from these types of investments.

There are many real-world situations where people can use zero coupon bonds. A basic example is a parent saving money for his or her child's college fund. It is easy to invest money that will mature by the time a child is college age. This will help pay for the cost of college. Another real-world example is wealthy people using zero coupon bonds to leave as an inheritance for family members. These beneficiaries do not have to pay as much tax as they would if it was not a bond.

Sometimes, zero coupon bonds are tax exempt, especially those issued by a government agency. Meanwhile, those issued by a corporation are not tax exempt. For these kinds of bonds, you will have to pay income tax for earnings that you have not yet received.

In the next section, we will look at mutual funds in detail.

What are Mutual Funds?

Mutual funds are schemes where a company will pool the money that it collects from several investors and then invest this money in the market. The company will not look for any one type of investment, and it will decide to put the investment wherever lucrative options are available. However, if there are common interests among the investors like "just stocks" or "just bonds," then it is possible for the mutual fund manager to invest in those particular securities alone.

Mutual fund returns are based on luck. Although companies will promise to give you back your money along with a profit, this is not always the case. Once the money is put into the market, units will be allotted to the individual investors. If you wish to invest in it, then you must understand all the risks that come with it.

Advantages of Investing in Mutual Funds

The advantage of mutual funds is that you can have a diversified portfolio. You can ask the fund manager to invest your money in different securities and help you get dividends, interest, and other forms of capital gain. This will also reduce your risk per security. You can calculate the net asset value at the end of the day. There is also the advantage of not having to monitor things personally, as the manager will make the best decisions for you. However, if you want, it is easier to compare these funds with others so you can work with your manager to make wise investments.

Moreover, mutual funds are quite profitable in the second market, which makes it a very valuable asset to have in your portfolio. Most mutual funds have tax advantages as well, which is great as you will keep more of your investment profit.

Disadvantages of Investing in Mutual Funds

The disadvantage of investing in mutual funds is that the companies charge a large amount as fees. This will be much more than your broker will charge you. Many of these fees are based on the fund type and the fund's risk level. If you are interested in day trading, then mutual funds would not be the right choice for you. There might be a small delay in the mutual fund investment, and if you miss out on buying the stocks you were interested in, then your mutual fund investment will be a waste.

Mutual funds are great choices for anyone interested in investing for a long time. There is no point in making an investment today and expecting the results tomorrow. Whether it is the stock market or mutual funds, you need to wait on it for it to grow in value. There are mutual funds that vary in size and investment time. Three to four years is the minimum investment time for mutual funds, but shorter terms are available, but these will not pay you a great return.

Mutual fund investments are of two types, namely, open-ended and close-ended funds. Open-ended funds are those that enable investors to access their investment and receive regular returns on it. Close-ended funds, on the other hand, are fixed and will not provide investor access. They are locked in and will not provide investors with any regular income. Investors can look at their net asset value at the end of the day, and that's about it. However, when the mutual fund reaches maturity, the investors can get all the benefits at once.

Another problem is inflation, which can be problematic when it rises. If you want to avoid inflation problems, it is better to avoid mutual funds and stick to stocks, as stocks have the ability to beat inflation. It is great to remember that like all investments, mutual funds are unpredictable, as inflation can lessen the value of the bond.

In the next section, we will look at the types of mutual funds that exist to help you make your choice.

Income Funds

The first type of mutual funds is quite popular and known as income funds. As the name suggests, they are used to derive a regular income and are thus employed as an investment scheme to end up with a fixed income on a monthly basis. A mutual fund never sticks to any one kind of investment and helps in diversifying your risk. So when it comes to income funds, the mutual fund scheme will not limit itself to just one kind of investment. It will look for several inner compositions for all its varieties. Thus, income funds will also be split up, and the fund manager will invest a person's money in all of its varieties. These varieties are given below.

Real estate investment trusts. A real estate investment trust is one in which the shareholders are paid a regular income for the real estate investments they make. This means that the shareholder is contributing towards the building and upkeep of real estate ventures, such as shopping malls, metros, office spaces, etc. Whatever the trust earns is split up and distributed to the shareholders. These shareholders will, therefore, derive a fixed sum of money from such investments.

Master limited partnerships. Master limited partnerships are those holdings where the company diversifies into separate subsidiaries. It will then allot the shareholder units that will comprise all the different subsidiaries. The shareholder will get paid whatever is earned by the different subsidiaries on a monthly basis.

Royalty trusts. Royalty trusts, such as the U.S. royalty trust, pay their shareholders money on a regular basis. These trusts will hold enterprises, such as oil and gas. However, this type has seen a sharp decline in the past few years, and mutual fund managers refrain from investing their shareholders' money in such trusts. Government bond investments are seen as being safer options than private investments. This is mainly because they are sure of not going bad, and even if they do, the government will ensure that all the shareholders receive their money.

The main advantage is the dividends that investors receive. However, there are disadvantages as well. It takes longer to see any returns, as the profits from the investment are used to give dividends but not investment growth. Another important risk is the chance of interruptions, which means that the issuer, for whatever reason, cannot make dividends. It's important to see if this fund is worth the risk for you.

Balanced Funds

A balanced fund is a hybrid mutual fund. It combines three to four different elements of financial securities. It takes a few stocks, some bond or income funds, as well as a few market investments and then prepares a combined portfolio. The idea of a balanced fund is to help investors diversify both their risk and income gain. Thus, by having a balanced fund, investors can have a regular income and remain invested for a long time. Balanced funds are great options for all the beginners looking to increase their financial holdings and diversifying their investments, as these funds are very simple. They are very easy to understand, as this type of fund is just balancing the risks and rewards of investing.

The general rule is to have 60% as your fixed investment and 40% as your regular income investment. The choice is yours, and you can select a combination that works for you, but remember that there will be a minimum investment clause, and you will have to invest whatever is expected of you.

There is the option of changing up the portfolio mix from time to time. This means that it is not necessary to hold on to the same kind of investment for long. If you feel like a particular aspect of your balanced fund mix is not working for you, then you can change it to something else that works in your favor. This kind of freedom is not available for other forms of mutual fund investments. Your fund manager will keep you updated on your incomes and also let you choose whether you stay or take an exit on the fund. In most cases, the manager himself will take a call on whether to exit a fund or not. He will keep switching it up depending on market conditions and how the economy is moving.

Like all investments, it has disadvantages, such as the manager fee being the same no matter how the market is performing. Moreover, it is not recommended to those who are in a lower tax bracket, as returns are very moderate, so to see a large return, you will need to invest a lot of money.

Equity Funds

Equity funds are another type of investment that the mutual fund encompasses. Here, there are three distinct qualities that the mutual fund manager looks at, namely, growth, value, and a mixture of the two. When you invest in an equity fund, you are looking at the growth of the company that you are investing in and their holding. This refers to how significantly the investment will grow over the course of time and what dividends the company will pay once it makes it big. Value refers to how valuable it will get over time or if it already is a big company. So you are looking for these both individually and as a combined output.

There are large cap options, mid cap options, and small cap options. It is entirely up to you to decide where you want to invest. Say, for example, you choose a well-established company that has a large business but does not have a good share price; this will be considered a large value investment. Conversely, say you invest in a company that has only limited finances owing to being a startup, but its share price is doing well in the market; you would call it a small growth investment.

The idea is to have some combined investments. All of them will add up to give you a combined profit in the end. The fund manager will suggest the best options that you can consider for your investment, as he or she will have a proper idea of what investment will pay off and how. However, as the ultimate investor, it is important for you to make the choice for yourself and not solely rely on the manager's suggestions. If you have done your research and know which stocks will do well, then you can suggest these to the manager and listen to his or her advice.

A great advantage of equity funds is that these funds have a great liquid value in the secondary market, so if you sell these funds, you can make a great profit. Another advantage is that managers do not charge large commission fees. It is important to check whether or not your manager will charge you a large fee for their services.

Global Funds

Global or international funds are a unique type of mutual fund investments. They are not to be used interchangeably, as both of them stand for different types of investments.

An international fund is one where the investment is compulsorily made in a country that is outside your home country. A global fund, on the other hand, is made anywhere in the world and might also include your home country. Overall, these are funds that are not limited to your state or region alone. Thus, confusing the two would be a mistake, and international funds can be considered as being bigger than global funds.

For example, a foreign currency investment is not necessarily a global fund. Foreign currency implies that you are investing in a currency that is not your own, but it is possible to invest in your own currency in certain situations. Let's say that a Texas-based investor is investing in Japanese currency, and only Japanese currency. That means that the Texan is investing in a foreign fund that would be considered an international fund instead of a global one because the investor is only investing in one foreign currency and not including his or her own, which is the U.S. dollar.

The main aim of having this type of fund is diversification. You know how important it is for your funds to be diversified in the stock market. If you invest in global or international funds, you have the chance to invest in a unique fund that will give you good returns. You will tap not only into the potential of your own market but also into the market of countries that might be financially stronger than yours. Now imagine having the chance to convert all your local currency into that of a country with currency that is trailing. You will obviously come into a bigger profit.

These types of funds are popular but undoubtedly quite risky, owing to a lack of proper knowledge and inefficiency in predicting global markets. It is quite tough to tame your local market, and it will be that much tougher to tame foreign markets. Your fund manager will have to conduct a lot of research in order to nest your money in this type of fund. The returns, however, will be well worth the effort, and you might end up making double or triple whatever you are already making in your local markets.

Specialty Funds

A specialty fund is a type of mutual funds that does not adhere to the common description of mutual funds. This means that they are quite unique and concentrate on a few sectors of the market. They can be classified as follows:

Sector funds. Sector funds, as the name suggests, pertain to those funds that are invested in certain specific sectors alone. These can include the technology sector, the financial sector, the health sector, fast-moving consumer goods, etc. All these sectors are separated, and the fund manager will decide to invest in the one that he or she thinks will throw up a lucrative output. The manager will not consult the client in general, as he or she will have access to the best information in the business. It is also advisable not to waste time in communicating with the clients, as the markets are extremely volatile, and every second counts.

Region-specific funds. As the name suggests, region-specific funds look at investments in a particular region of the world, be it local or foreign. The idea is to incorporate a foreign investment into the portfolio. This is possible only if the person is eligible for foreign investment. The manager will have to do some amount of research and understand the markets thoroughly. There is a certain amount of risk associated with these types of funds, and the investor should be made fully aware of these before the investment goes through. The most risk to undertake will arise if the foreign country goes into a recession.

Social responsibility funds. These are funds where the manager will avoid investing in companies that indulge in illegal businesses. These can include arms and ammunition building, import and export of banned substances, etc. If these companies get into trouble, then the investor's money will be in trouble. Moreover, it is the responsibility of the investor to not promote such trade for the betterment of society.

A huge disadvantage of this fund is the fact that there is a risk of lack of portfolio diversity because you are investing in a specialized fund. While you can invest in different specialized markets, it does not mean you have a greater chance of making a profit whether you invest in one specialized market or two.

Mutual Insurance

As stated briefly in the "Insurance Shares" section of the previous chapter, a mutual insurance company, sometimes known as a mutual insurance fund, is an insurance company that is mainly owned by policyholders.

The advantage of this fund is the fact that it exists to make sure that the benefits promised to the policyholders are there for the long term. This means that policyholders can make decisions that will benefit them in the long run. The main disadvantage is that members are charged a premium so the company can make a profit.

This premium is like an investment because policyholders have an option of receiving either a dividend or lower premiums. This is an advantage and is the best part of paying premiums.

While mutual insurance is not similar to either of the funds in this section, it is important to mention it so as to separate it from insurance shares. Interestingly enough, a mutual insurance can become publicly traded if expenses have risen. In such situation, all the policyholders will become shareholders.

An example of a mutual insurance company is Liberty Mutual Insurance, which is policyholder owned and covers many different insurance needs, such as home, life, and car insurance. It differs from the likes of MetLife, Aflac, and Progressive, which only focus on one or two aspects of insurance needs.

While this kind of fund might seem different from the other ones in this section, it is similar enough to seem important so that people will not confuse it with insurance shares.

Index Funds

Index funds, as the name suggests, refer to those funds that mimic the market indexes. Thus, if I were to formulate a portfolio, it would involve the various elements of the market index. It would be similar to condensing the market into my portfolio. Index funds are said to be independent and do not really fall under the category of mutual funds. However, for ease of understanding and practical application, they are added under mutual funds.

The main idea is to flow with the market and match its footsteps. This can be a difficult task if people do not understand how to interpret the market. The fund manager will assist in the process and explain the various elements that make up the market. The investor can then choose the different elements that comprise the portfolio.

The management fees that these types of investments require are much lower than those required by regular mutual funds, so they are a good option for all those looking to come into a good profit without having to shell out a lot of money towards mutual fund fees. The reason why these fees are lower is that managers are not as active with index funds as they are with other types of investment funds. Studies have shown that this type of fund beats actively managed funds over time.

Despite some of the advantages of index funds, there are some disadvantages. These disadvantages include a lack of flexibility because these funds are dependent on the stock market. Moreover, index funds, at best, only give average returns because there is no opportunity to outperform the market, as market indexes are based on an average of certain factors of the markets.

These form the various types of mutual funds that exist in the market, and you can choose one depending on your investment plan and how much money you have at your disposal.

Chapter 4: Investing In Etfs And Precious Metals

By now, we have looked at stocks/shares, options, bonds, and mutual funds in detail. In this chapter, we will learn about exchange-traded funds (ETFs) and precious metals as options for you to invest in.

What are ETFs?

Exchange-traded funds, better known as ETFs, are investment funds that are listed and traded in the stock exchange. They basically work like stocks and bonds and are held over the course of the day. ETFs can be compared to mutual funds, but they are traded all through the day. They are bought and sold in the stock exchange, and the investor will make a profit or loss depending on how the underlying security has fared. It is basically saying you have asked your broker to treat your investment as a mutual fund. For instance, you invest in stocks, bonds, and future securities and make them a unit. You can then put this unit in the market for sale. Thus, you have the convenience of both a mutual fund and a stock.

There are lower fees than a mutual fund and higher daily liquidity like common stocks. Unlike a mutual fund, the net asset value (NAV) is not calculated at the end of the day.

Advantages of Investing in ETFs

The advantage of ETFs is that they have low expense ratios as compared to traditional mutual funds. Mutual funds are not ideal for low investors because of their high expense ratios. These investors thus opt for ETFs instead. ETFs are highly liquid, and investors do not have to wait for the end of the day to calculate their net asset value. They are traded all through the day at the stock exchange. There is lesser tax liability, as trading in ETFs will not invite capital gains tax. You also have the option of trading them like stocks, which gives them far more flexibility.

Disadvantages of Investing in ETFs

The disadvantage of ETFs is that the securities that ETFs track are always fixed. This means that if someone wishes to manage his or her ETF and tries to mix up the portfolio, it won't be possible. The dividends that an investor gains from ETF investments will not be as high as high-yielding stocks. In fact, a person might have to invest for 10 to 15 years and patiently wait for the overall value to grow, which is not feasible for intraday traders.

One thing to remember here is that you will always remain the indirect owner of the underlying asset and not the direct one. This means that you will never have 100% possession of the assets that the ETF stands for. It is possible for you to deal with it on an intraday basis as well, but the prices will not rise and fall steeply.

Different Types of ETFs

The great thing about ETFs is that there are many types that an investor can choose from. However, some are more popular than others. The following section shows some of the more popular ETFs that people invest in.

Foreign ETF

A foreign ETF shows that the countries that have an exchange also produce ETFs. This ETF is great for those who want exposure to an international market and for those who want to hedge risks with foreign investing. Examples of Foreign ETFs include AFK (Market Vectors Africa), UXJ (Ultra MSCI Pacific Ex-Japan), AUD (Australia Bond Index Fund), and FXB (Currency Shares British Pound Sterling Trust).

There are many advantages to this type of ETF. These include foreign exposure, a diverse portfolio, and risk management. These advantages are great because foreign exposure helps build your portfolio and makes it as diverse as it can be, and having a diverse portfolio is a great thing. However, there are many disadvantages to this ETF. Taxes comprise a big one because every country has their own tax laws. Just because ETFs are tax exempt in the United States doesn't mean that they are also exempt in another country like Canada or Belgium.

Currency rates can also lead to problems if there is a big difference between any two currencies. For example, if the U.S. dollar is way higher than the Euro, then it might lead to problems with returns for an investor. Moreover, ETFs are not flexible, and foreign ETFs are not an exception.

Alan Anderson

It is also very important that you research foreign ETFs before investing so that you can avoid some of the disadvantages. For example, if you notice a difference between one currency and another, then it is not a great idea to invest in that foreign ETF.

Foreign Currency ETF

Just like you can invest in foreign markets, you can also invest in foreign currency itself. This is great for people who want to make foreign investments but want to avoid the futures market. This type of ETF needs to be researched thoroughly, as there are both great advantages and disadvantages. Most major currencies are available to invest in, such as UDN (Power Shares US Dollar Bearish) and GDAY (ProShares UltraShort Australian Dollar).

There are many advantages to this kind of ETF. Aside from gaining exposures, it is easy and inexpensive to trade foreign currency. Moreover, if there are any fluctuations between currencies, you can make a profit.

However, transactions of foreign currency can become quite complex, and unless you really understand the futures market, things might get confusing. Furthermore, those with better math skills have an advantage over those who don't because they can use math to see potential returns.

Volatility ETFs

In certain situations, having a volatility ETF can be great, while in other times, it can seem like a bad investment. The reason is that the lower the volatility, the more the ETF is worth, and the same is true for the opposite situation. If the ETF is low, then the volatility is high. As long as you pay attention to the market, then this ETF can make you a profit.

There are certain graphs and stock research that can help with this type of ETF. If you look at the S&P 500 index, it can show you when to buy and sell. If the VXX (the volatility) is in the lead in the charts, then you should check where the color lines are located. If the red line is low and the yellow line is high, then that is a good indicator about the ETF, but if the opposite is true, then the volatility has risen.

That being said, a great advantage of this ETF is that it is perfect for day traders as the price swings are high, which means there is a chance for a high return. It is important to use stop orders as this ETF is unpredictable at times, and no method can guarantee a positive outcome all the time.

Sector and Industry ETFs

Sector and industry ETFs are very similar to indexes, as they have same securities and similar assets. However, the difference is that the ETF is tracking the industry index, and it is trying to mimic – not outperform – the industry index. This ETF is great for those who want exposure in a certain industry and who want to do it all in one transaction. Those who want a hedged risk will also benefit from industry and sector ETFs.

The industries and sectors included in this ETF are energy, consumer goods, industrials, information technology, and telecommunications.

There are many advantages to this type of ETF. It is great for following sectors, as you can compare the ETF and index for a given sector to see how it is performing. Another advantage is that you avoid the disadvantages associated with index trading, such as the expected prices being higher or lower.

Most brokers charge a lower commission fee with this ETF, and it is a great building block for your portfolio, especially if you are starting to build one. However, there are many disadvantages as well because there is no flexibility at all with this ETF and all ETFs in general. However, the main disadvantage is that you are at the mercy of your issuer when you want to adjust your shares because of the inflexible nature of ETFs.

How Does ETF Differ From ETN

An exchanged traded note (ETN) can be considered the ETF's unknown cousin. Everyone knows what an ETF is in investment, but many investors have never heard of an ETN. ETF and ETN are similar in practice as they track underlying assets, and their expense ratios are lower when they are compared to actively managed mutual funds. Moreover, they both trade on major exchanges like their stocks.

However, they are very different, as one is a mixture of a stock and fund, while the other is like a bond.

An ETF is the mixture of a stock and a fund. It tracks assets that are associated with the funds. There are many examples of ETFs, such as gold, futures, bonds, and stocks. These assets are easy to track. In fact, it is easy to buy and trade most of these assets in most situations. Moreover, these are the assets that most people associate with the stock exchange. While there are many advantages and disadvantages to ETF, it is useful when you want to expand your portfolio.

Meanwhile, ETNs are like bonds, but the debt associated with them is unsecured as it is not issued by an institution like the government. Many ETNs are issued by banks, and this is the reason why you can invest in foreign currencies with ETNs rather than ETFs. ETNs' bond-like quality stems from the fact that like bonds, ETNs can be bought and sold whether the investor decides for the bond to reach maturity or not.

However, there are some major disadvantages to ETNs. For example, if a bank (banks being the main issuers of ETNs) goes bankrupt, then the investor might risk being in total default. Moreover, the credit rating of the issuer is important because the shares go down once the issuer has a credit downgrade, regardless of the product that it is tracking. Another disadvantage is that ETN does not rely on buying and selling assets, so it only pays once the fund has matured. Nevertheless, an advantage of ETN is that there are no tracking errors, so you know exactly how your bond is doing in the markets.

Research is very important to see if an ETN is better for your investing needs, as it is very different and riskier than ETF. It is not usually recommended for new investors to get into the ETN market because there are more risks than rewards. This is what separates ETN from ETFs. In certain ETFs like precious metals, you do not have to wait for full maturity to see a return.

What are Precious Metals?

Gold and silver have been regarded as some of the most precious metals in the world, and they still hold their position to this day. Although their value fluctuates all through the year, they will never become useless or obsolete.

There are a few precious metals that regular investors invest in to increase the scope of their portfolios. These include gold, silver, and platinum. Although there are other metals that are available for trade, including copper, zinc, and lead, these are not necessarily precious and are suited for intraday trading.

Unlike stocks and other securities, it is impossible to predict how the market will perceive the value of these precious metals. There are no companies involved on whose performance we could base the value of these metals. Thus, it becomes extremely tough to say when and why people will start buying and hoarding them or start selling them.

Precious metals are traded on the bullion market. The bullion market is a mostly London-based, over-the-counter market that is open 24 hours a day. This market deals primarily in gold and silver.

However, based on experience, it is safe to assume that the following factors will impact the value of precious metals:
- When there is rampant instability in banks and rates and the political scenario is changing the face of the government constantly, then it will be difficult for you to trust these institutions with your money and so, precious metals will make for safe bets.

- When there is instability in the stock market and stock prices are plummeting, then people will turn to precious metals to help safeguard their monetary investments.

Remember that this investment is specifically for gold and silver bars and coins and not necessarily the jewelry made out of them (although that is also an option). Jewelry will be marked up owing to making costs and wastages, and people will get less precious metal for the same price. However, that should not stop you from buying these, as they will also be considered as being precious metal investments.

Advantages of Investing in Precious Metals

The advantage of investing in precious metals is that they are not affected by inflation. So if stocks and other securities are going down owing to inflation, metal value will not plummet and will remain stable. The value of precious metals will be universal in nature. That is, they will have a global value, which is universal and can be flexibly traded across the globe. Unlike other forms of securities, you become the full and final owner of these metals once you buy them. Remember, the gold, silver, or platinum you have today will always have a higher value tomorrow. If you buy it at rate X today, and it is valued at rate Y tomorrow, then Y will always be greater than X. However, this tomorrow might be a couple to a several years later.

Other advantages include a diverse portfolio and the fact you can physically own your investment as precious metals are tangible. There is also variety in this investment as precious metals can be used in many projects, such as appliance production and minting coins. In fact, this is one of the few investments that you can take home with you as you can get the physical investments like bars, coins, and jewelry delivered to your home. This type of investment is great for those who want to invest into something that is long-term and relativity safe. Despite the security of this investment, there are still some disadvantages.

Disadvantages of Investing in Precious Metals

The major disadvantage of this type of investment is that the initial investment will be quite large. You cannot buy a gold biscuit while having a small budget. You will need a substantial amount to buy a substantial amount of gold. You will also not receive any regular returns on your investments, like dividends or interests, on your precious metals. Moreover, there are huge costs, such as duty taxes, if you want to own your investment in a physical form, such as coins or bars, as many people like to have these items in their home.

A big disadvantage is that theft can happen if you own a physical investment because precious metals are worth a lot, no matter where they are sold. Even if the person who stole your investment sold it on the black market, they could make a large amount of money from it. Another disadvantage is that this is a long-term investment, so if you do not hold on to this investment for a long time, the prices will work against you, as you would not make any money if you let go of it too soon. Furthermore, you need to make sure that you have enough money to pay the extra fee associated with precious metals, such as commission fees from your broker and any taxes that might have to be paid as well.

The following are various precious metals to choose from:

Gold

The first precious metal we will focus on is gold. It is obvious that you have heard of this metal and also know how valuable it truly is. Since time immemorial, gold has been bought and sold as a valuable item. Ever since gold was discovered, people understand that it is a scarce commodity and something that cannot be exploited.

You must have seen your mother, aunts, sisters, etc., buy gold jewelry. Whether the piece is a ring or a necklace, they will make sure they get the best price and also check the quality of gold. They will look at the shine and the weight of the metal. All these are indicators of the good quality of gold. Checking quality is as crucial as buying the gold itself. There can be a lot of frauds out there who will do all sorts of things, like coating bronze with a thin layer of gold and parading it as real gold. If you end up buying something like this, then rest assured that you will not be happy with your investment.

Apart from jewelry, gold is also used in various other industries, including the dental industry, electronic industry, and other such allied industries. Thus, it is always in demand, and its price will keep fluctuating all through the day, day after day. If you wish to buy gold today, then you have to check whether the price has dropped or risen since yesterday. If the price has dropped, then you must buy it immediately, but if it has risen, then consider waiting a little longer to see if the price drops again. If you think it is steadily rising, then don't worry; it will fall sometime soon, but if you don't want to wait, then you can buy it immediately.

Apart from these factors, hoarders greatly control the price in the market. They will buy lots of gold in bulk, as they will have the resources to buy it and then hoard it. This will cause the gold rate to rise, as there will be less gold available in the market. Subsequently, when the hoarder decides to sell all his possessions, the gold rate will simply drop. Thus, you will see a sharp decline in the rate of gold. This keeps happening day in and day out, and the price of gold will never be stable. However, one thing is for sure: if you buy gold today for $500, you can expect to sell it at a much higher price in a year's time. This kind of guarantee is what makes this metal highly desirable.

If you invest in gold ETFs, there are some advantages. Similar to all gold investments, there is good liquidity, and it is easy to sell. However, unlike investing in physical gold that you can have in your home, there is no VAT, service tax, and wealth tax that you will have to pay. However, there are disadvantages as well. Owing to manager fees, ETFs in gold are more expensive than investing in actual gold. Another disadvantage is that gold ETFs might become popular. Popularity can cause everyone to buy investments, which will reduce the price of the ETF. However, given that there are many different ways to invest in gold, the low price may not be a big thing, as gold is in many different markets.

Silver

Silver is the next precious metal that makes for a good investment. As you know, both gold and silver are traded on a regular basis. They are both precious and used in the jewelry business. However, silver finds more industrial use than gold, which makes it a better investment option. Silver is in demand in many markets, such as the superconductor and microcircuit markets, because silver is used in batteries. Moreover, there is a demand for more household appliances in the Eastern markets, as the middle class is growing in this region.

There will be a lot of fluctuations in its price, and at no time will silver's rate remain constant. The price fluctuates because it swings because it is a tangible item used in industry and because of its store value. Silver is more volatile than gold because of this.

Silver is more widely available than gold, so it is preferred as an investment option. You will have the chance to buy more silver at any given time and hoard it if you like. You can then slowly begin to release it back into the market and start affecting the price. Many people adopt this strategy to affect the price of silver. They will buy it at a certain price, wait for its value to rise, and then sell everything that they have. This will cause the price to fall, and so, they will again invest in some amount. They will keep doing this until they have had their fill. Thus, this is a great investment for contrarians who want to add precious metals into their portfolio, as this method is very much like the one contrarians use.

However, they will not be interested in possessing any silver at all and will only keep playing with its prices. In this way, they can be compared to regular intraday traders. Conversely, those keenly interested in buying silver can consider buying it when it is priced at its lowest and then hoard it for a long time.

Many factors affect the price of silver. Apart from industrial requirements, many tournaments that award gold and silver medals will end up affecting the price of silver. This will cause a steep rise in its prices, so it is a good time to sell your silver if you think a major tournament is approaching. For example, if it is near the Olympics – either the summer or the winter, maybe even both – you can turn a profit by selling some of your silver.

However, silver is not as valuable as gold. Its market rate will be much lower than that of gold. So even if you sell your silver, you will not make a big profit out of it. Thus, hoarding it or selling it when its price has steeply risen will be the only option that you have with silver. It's important to know that the price of silver is based on its applications, so its price differs in the different markets that use silver.

Again, you can turn it into jewelry or cutlery and still retain a profit.

Platinum

Platinum is possibly the priciest of all precious metals. Platinum is extremely pricey owing to its rarity and luster. It is much brighter and shinier than gold or silver and has a brilliant sparkle to it.

Like gold and silver, platinum is traded in the bullion market. It is always on the higher levels owing to its diverse use in both industrial and non-industrial applications. The jewelry industry also thrives on this precious metal and considers it an important part of bullion trade.

The reason why platinum is rare and in high demand is because of its concentration in just two countries in the world, one of them being Russia and the other being South Africa. These two countries mine the metal and export all over the world. There are many instances of rampant illegal cartels, which further affect the cost of this metal. So it is important to understand that this metal is extremely volatile, and the prices will surge and plummet in a matter of minutes. If you are serious about trading in precious metals, then you must keep an eye on the prices all through the day.

For example, those who invest in jewelry know that platinum jewelry is always more expensive than silver and gold. In some situations, platinum might be worth more than diamonds. However, diamonds are dependent on numerous factors, such as color, weight, and cut. However, as stated previously, platinum is the rarest precious metal in the world. That is why platinum is very valuable and worth the investment, no matter your income bracket.

Precious metals are a great investment choice for you, and you can choose the one that fits your budget. However, even a choosy investor will try to incorporate all three of these metals into his or her portfolio. You can do the same. You need not buy a lot of everything and can have just a small quantity of each allotted into your portfolio.

However, make sure you make the best of what you have, and use it in your life instead of simply hoarding it.

Alan Anderson

Chapter 5: Social Media Stocks

In this chapter, we will discuss and take a brief look at a new trend in stocks, social media, as we shift away from ETFs and precious metals.

What is Social Media?

Social media is an umbrella term referring to websites and apps that let users post, create, and share content. Most people use this to connect with friends, families, and colleagues in both the personal and professional aspects of their lives. People do so by posting status updates, pictures, and videos about their interests, their vacations, etc.

Like most people, you probably have or had a Facebook account. Facebook is an example of a social media site in which people can post about their lives, or they can use it for their businesses. However, social media is becoming increasingly important to our world, as people use it for more than keeping up with friends. Businesses use it to connect with consumers, and professionals use it to network, which places it in high demand.

So many people around the world are starting to use these sites and apps so much that they need to make money other than through their ad revenues and initial investments when the companies were startups. Many of these websites are starting to go public and attract more investors.

What is Social Media Stock?

It should be first noted that not every social media company is publicly traded, so you cannot buy stocks for every social media platform that you use. However, some of the big social media sites are public, and you can buy stocks for these companies. Facebook and Twitter are some of the big names in the stock market. In some cases, a bigger company that may or may not have anything to do with the social media market will buy out a social media platform and put it under its own stock.

Social media stock, like social media itself, features many companies that are available to purchase stocks and shares. These include social gaming developers like Net Ease and business review sites like Yelp. You can also invest in companies that own social websites like Yahoo, which owns Flickr and Tumblr, and Google, which owns YouTube and developed its own social media platform, Google+. Researching the topic can help you find out whether a publicly traded company owns a current social media site or if a social media site has its own IPO.

Not every social media stock is for a company based in the U.S. Due to laws concerning internet restriction in China, many Chinese companies have developed their own versions of popular social media sites like Facebook. In fact, China has publicly traded companies that you can invest in; for example, Weibo Corporation is a social media platform. Another example is Changyou.com, which is a social gaming platform.

As you can see, there are numerous companies that you can buy stock for, and the list keeps growing. As social media becomes a part of our lives, more companies will either buy social media sites or the sites themselves will become publicly traded companies.

It is important for investors to research and figure out whether investing in social media stocks will be great for their portfolio and worth the investment.

Advantages of Social Media

The main advantage of buying social media stock is that everyone uses it. From this standpoint, it can be an easy way to make a profit because only the widely used websites go public without being bought by another company. The reason is that they can find enough investors to keep it as its own independent company because projected growth can show investors that it is worth the risk for a great profit. For example, this is the reason why Facebook is a public company, whereas Tumblr has only technically become a public company since Yahoo bought it. Another advantage is that website growth is easy to track, which is useful as these sites only make money when their growth continues and if they don't lose any users.

Social media companies can buy other social media companies as well. For example, Facebook owns Instagram, so when you buy Facebook stock, you are also buying stock for other social media platforms like Instagram. This is great for investors, as it shows that companies like Facebook make enough profits that it can buy other companies. A growth of profits means more dividends to those who bought shares of the company. It also shows how social media can be a great investment.

Name recognition is also advantageous in this market, as it makes easier to see how it works. This is great for investors that use fundamental trading because their research is easier as they would just look at the site as an example. Moreover, this type of stock is great for those who want a diverse portfolio, as social media stock can be risky at times. However, the huge returns can be worth this risk.

Moreover, name recognition makes the company seem more trustworthy among new investors. As investors know the name, then they know the brand. If the investors know and like the brand, then they are more willing to invest in the social media stock. Although it is recommended that new investors, mainly those new to the stock market, stay away from social media stock because of the risks.

Disadvantages of Social Media

Despite the fact that we all use it, there are a lot of disadvantages of social media as well, the main one being that most social media companies have a short life span. It is very easy for a company to lose users to competitors and thus lose profit. An example of this is when Facebook took over Myspace in the late '00s.

Although Myspace never went public itself, News Corporation bought the company in 2005 after the website started to become extremely popular with young people. However, by 2009, many of Myspace's users went over to Facebook, and the company started to lose money. In 2011, New Corporation cut their losses and sold the company. Meanwhile, Facebook is still popular, and it has its own IPO. Thus, if the social media company does not keep itself current, growing and keeping its users, you will lose any potential profit. It also shows how social media platforms are fickle, and it is rare for one to last more than a few years.

Aside from the short life span, another disadvantage is that many of these stocks are over hyped. This means that a large number of people will buy these stocks, thinking that they will make a short-term profit, but sometimes, it is quite the opposite. Depending on how the company does, you either make a small profit, or you lose money. Moreover, there are many risks in investing in social media sites, as these platforms are dependent on user growth.

While name recognition seems like an advantage, in some cases, it is a disadvantage. People who are new to the stock market are always told to invest in companies that they know. It was given as advice in Chapter 1 and at least a few other times after that. However, social media is a very risky stock for anyone to invest in, especially brand new investors, as they are often unaware of the dangers of risky stocks. Someone new to investing could invest in this kind of stock and lose profits really fast.

Is Investing in Social Media Risky?

Yes, it is very risky. As mentioned above, social media stock depends on such factors as user growth and decline. Given that technology changes rapidly, companies have to be quick to adapt. Not only do these companies have to adapt to technology, but they also have to adapt to the needs of users. Failure to do so can lead people to seek out a competitor, and it can cause users to find competitors and tell everyone they know about any competition. If the company loses users, they not only lose money, but it can also affect their market value because people are going to sell their stock.

Another risk is that many of these websites have a short life, as it depends on how long the platform and/or the company stay popular. Like all things that are very popular, most of these platforms will slowly decline and never rise above this. That is the main risk of social media stock – it not a long-term investment most of the time, which is terrible for those who like to buy and hold their stocks. Social media stocks are only great for a short-term investment.

However, there are people who believe that social media stock is a bubble waiting to burst. If you would like to minimize your risks, then stay away from social media stock in case it is a bubble. There will be more on that at the end of this chapter.

Is the Stock Market the Only Way to Invest in Social Media?

No. There are a lot of ways to invest in a social media company. The least risky way – in the stock market – is to invest in a company that is not a social media giant but owns a social media platform. As mentioned earlier, both Yahoo and Google own social media platforms. This is a great way because your stocks would not be as affected by user decline as it would if you had invested in a social media company outright.

However, an important way to invest aside from the markets is to do so when the company is a startup. By startup, we refer to when the company is at the earlier stages of development and is not widely known yet.

What is a Social Media Startup?

To begin, we have to explain what a startup company is. A startup is an entrepreneurial company that is trying to get into the marketplace by developing an innovative project or offering an innovative service that is unique. To a social media startup, their app or website is offering something that you cannot get on the other social media platforms. Developers are trying to get the platform off the ground to make their product available to the public as an app, a website, or both. This means developers are going to need investments to help pay for business costs, such as paying for your app to be in an app store (which varies for Apple and Google).

Anyone can make a social media startup. In fact, some of the most creative social media platforms came from out of nowhere. For example, the app Snapchat started as a project that the creators had made for a class at Stanford. However, it also leads to a higher risk, as investors have to tell if a platform has a chance of making it big because not every platform will be the next YouTube or Twitter.

Many people question whether social media is worth the risk and some financial advisors will be against investing in startups, as the risk is greater than the reward most of the time.

Why Do People Invest in Startups?

There are many reasons why people invest in startups. Some people really believe that their new investment will be the next YouTube or Instagram. Others think that their investment will be returned because they assume that all young people use apps. Whatever the reason, some people think that this investment is worth the risks.

You don't have to invest in startups. As mentioned above, it is not recommended that you invest in startups because they are very risky. The reason this section is in this chapter is for information on how people invest in social media platforms. However, if you have the money to risk and you want to invest in a startup, go ahead. But remember to do research about the market. For example, if you want to invest in an app that is going to compete with YouTube, then you need to research YouTube and your potential investment, as you need to see how the investment differs from YouTube. You will also need to know if there are any complaints YouTube users have and see if your potential investment will meet this demand that Google is ignoring.

However, most YouTube competition will never be as good as YouTube because Google is great at addressing any problems that one might have with their social media platforms. This is a perfect example of the risks associated with startups, as explained below.

Startups Risks

There are a lot of people who have startups. In fact, it may seem daunting to find a company that will succeed. That is the risk; not every startup will be a Snapchat, as most startups will not guarantee a profit. Most startup investors have a lot of money to spend on these investments because startups need to raise large amounts of money to avoid being bought by another bigger company. Thus, this investment is not wise for those who are not in the higher tax brackets, as the risk is too great, and a return may never happen.

Another risk is that the youth – mainly teens – might not use the startup's platform. A reason that many take the risk in investing is that if the platform becomes popular with teens, then everyone else will eventually start using the app. Thus, investors will eventually make a profit from the startup. If this app gets popular enough, another company will buy out the investors to own the platform. Alternatively, just like Facebook and Snapchat, the company will go public, which means investors get a bigger return if the stock does well.

However, not every platform will have this kind of success, but the risk, at times, may be worth it. It is important to research the market before investing in a startup to help minimize your risk because you can see if your potential investment has any competitors. Moreover, it is recommended that you talk to your financial advisor or portfolio manager to see if this investment is a great idea.

Is Social Media Investment the Future?

Yes and no. Yes in that this market is slowly becoming a way of life. So as long as there are social media platforms that are able to become IPOs, then there are always going to be stock for people to buy and trade. But no in that there will be a long-lasting company to buy stock from. I don't mean larger media companies that buy social networks like Yahoo or Google. I mean social platforms that have their own IPOs like Twitter. Given the short life span that most social media sites have, there is no guarantee that these platforms will be like Disney or Coca-Cola and have a lasting stay in the market. It is important to strategize in this market and figure out how long

Alan Anderson

you want to hold the stock before you sell or trade.

The only problem that social media stock has with longevity, outside of the short life span, is that many believe that this might be a bubble. In the stock market, a bubble is when investors drive the prices up above the actual value of the stock. Social media has shown characteristics associated with a stock bubble because many people are willing to buy this type of stock. A bubble could theoretically happen, but it does not mean it will happen. Like most stocks, you have to be careful of the risks. However, with social media stock, you have to be super careful, but a great investor can help you decide whether the risks are worth any potential returns.

Chapter 6: Brokers

The last chapter was about whether social media stocks are an important new market. In this chapter, we will go into more detail on brokers and their importance in helping you make investments.

The Different Types of Brokers

As mentioned in the first chapter, brokers are people who buy and sell securities (stocks, shares, bonds, etc.) via the stock and over-the-counter markets for a commission. However, in some situations, brokers sell non-securities to their clients. Just like there are different types of markets, there are different types of brokers. Many of these brokers work in different markets, and those who work in different investment markets have different functions from those in stocks. No matter the type of broker you choose, it is best to look for one who will help you with your investment goals.

Stock Broker

By now, we all know that the broker mentioned above is a stock broker. As stated earlier, stock brokers work for a commission, and these commissions usually cost around $15, but it differs for every stock broker, as some will charge more if they offer more services. Another thing about stock brokers is that most of them work on the floors of the stock exchange, although there are some who do so online. That being said, there are two types of stock brokers: discount and full-service brokers.

Full-service brokers perform a variety of services. They offer clients such things as advice, tax tips, and retirement planning tips, along with buying, trading, and selling stocks. These brokers are great for those who not only want to trade stocks but also want tax advice, among other financial advice and planning services. Full-service brokers have higher commission rates than a discount broker because of the other services offered. For those who do not have time to stay up-to-date with the stock market, this might be the way to go, especially if you can afford to pay the higher commission fee. Moreover, if you are a first-time investor, it is recommended that you use a full-service stock broker, as financial advice is part of the broker's services.

A discount broker is for those who want someone to buy and trade stocks without the bells and whistles that come with a full-service broker. Discount brokers do not offer any financial advice. However, their commission fees are lower than that of full-service brokers because they don't offer a lot of services, and many discount brokers are not busy with high profile clients because they usually work online and not physically at the exchange. Discount brokers are great for those who are active with their trades because using a discount broker does not take away from any profits earned. We will learn more about this type of stock broker later in this section.

Real Estate Broker

A real estate broker represents the seller of a given property. Real estate brokers do numerous duties, including determining market values, advertising properties on the market, showing off properties to potential buyers, and giving clients advice.

Although people think the term "real estate broker" can be used interchangeably with "real estate agent" and "Realtor," all three terms are completely different when you want to buy or sell real estate properties. Real estate agents have taken and passed a series of requirement classes and an exam that differs in each state. Meanwhile, Realtors are real estate agents that are members of NAR (National Association of Realtors) who have agreed to abide by the NAR's rules and code of ethics. A broker is a step above an agent and realtor and will have taken and passed an exam for brokers. The main difference is that a broker can work independently, while agents and realtors have to work under a licensed broker. So unlike the other investment markets, there is always going to be a broker around for advice even if you are using a realtor or agent.

Brokers can help you with any advice you need when you invest in real estate. This includes whether a property is worth the investment and property taxes that you will have to pay on your investment. Real estate brokers do charge a commission fee, which is usually around 6%. Before you hire a broker for any real estate needs, research the broker to see if he or she is worth the commission fee. You don't want to be overcharged if you don't think the broker is good, so if this is the case, try to negotiate the fee.

High-End Broker

High-End brokers work with researchers to study the condition of the economy and plan advice around the research that was found in the studies conducted. Thus, high-end brokers usually find and know trends, which they can give advice on to clients based on their research findings. For example, a high-end dealer that has a client with investments in the stock market can advise his or her client on when to buy and sell their stocks.

Just as the name suggests, a high-end broker works with wealthy clients. The fees for these brokers depend on the market, as high-end brokers can work in different sectors. However, the fee is most likely higher than the standard broker commission of a given sector, as the broker's work is more detailed and research-based because he or she is working with a research team.

An example of a high-end broker is the broker-dealer. A broker-dealer, from what we recall briefly from the first chapter, is a person that is both a broker and dealer for his or her firm. Given that broker-dealers also buy securities for themselves or their firm, they can also give advice and deals to their clients because they know current trends of the market, thanks to their firm's research team. High-end brokers are great for those who are investing in very expensive things, as it is more likely that they can afford the services of this type of broker.

Insurance Broker

Insurance is an interesting market. It should be noted that insurance brokers, while not mentioned as much as the content above, do have to be licensed as a financial broker as they may have a fiduciary duty to their companies and to anyone buying insurance. Companies need to know what a risk is or what is not a risk when giving out any type of insurance, so they will know what situations can be covered and which ones cannot. Meanwhile, buyers need to know what they are buying, how it works, and the risk of purchasing a given insurance, whether it is for health, car, or life.

If a mutual company has to offer an insurance share because the company's expenses were greater than the policyholders' premium payments total, the insurance broker will have to use his or her fiduciary duty because the company is now a part of the stock exchange.

Online Broker

An online broker is just a fancy name for a discount broker. The reason why there are two terms to describe the broker type is that in the American market, this kind of broker is referred to as a "discount broker," while in the rest of the world's markets, especially in Europe, the broker is known as an "online broker." While this seems confusing, it really is not. It is just useful to remember that the two terms are the same thing and that they can be used interchangeably, unlike the terms in the real estate section from earlier in this chapter.

As the name suggests and as mentioned earlier in this chapter, an online/discount broker does everything online. Even the brokerage firm is an online company. There is a wide range of brokerage firms to work with online. The best way to choose an online brokerage firm is to figure out which ones offer services to meet your investment needs. There is a chance that there are online reviews of these brokerage firms that can help you find one that meets your online trading needs. This is an advantage of an online broker because it is easier to find the right broker, as you can read reviews on the firm. However, a disadvantage is that you have to make sure that the brokerage firm is real and not an internet scam. You will learn more on this in the next section.

What to Look for in a Broker

If you are new to making investments, it is recommended that you not only hire a broker, but hire a full-service one. It is important to remember from Chapter 1 that a broker is not a financial advisor. To know that you are hiring a broker, you need to remember that a broker is licensed. Brokers have to have a license to sell and buy stocks, shares, and other investment opportunities for you. For example, an America-based broker will need to have a Financial Industry Regulatory Authority (FINRA) license to work.

Moreover, brokers work for firms, whether physical or online, that are members of organizations, such as FINRA or the Securities Investor Protection Corporation. Companies will always mention that they are certified and members of these organizations to potential investors that want to work with their firms. This is very important if you use an online broker, as you have to be more vigilant against scams and con artists online. Making use of online reviews and determining whether or not an online brokerage firm is real is made easier if you search to see if they are a member of organizations like FINRA.

There are also other things to look for, such as minimum price to start a brokerage account and withdrawal fees. A discount broker has a lower minimum than a full-service broker, for example. Some brokerage firms charge you a fee to withdraw your money, or they won't let you withdraw if your balance is below that minimum start price. It is important to check this out with any potential firms you might work with.

It is also important to figure out what type of investor you are, as different brokers are needed for different needs. For example, a long-term investor would do better with a trader, as it would minimize any fees, while a short-term investor would be better off with a broker, as they will be more concerned with trends and when to buy and sell stock.

Advantages of Having a Broker

There are many advantages to having a broker. For stock brokers, the main advantage is that the broker is focused on helping you make a profit. Stock brokers can also do some of the more boring aspects of investing for you, like keeping a record of all investments and other paperwork. Moreover, a stock broker manages your portfolio and can educate you on the markets. It doesn't matter if you are using a full-service, online (discount), or even a high-end one. You will still have someone who can help you when you need it.

Furthermore, a broker can be a gatekeeper for certain investments. Similar to real estate, you cannot get a property without working with a broker. In the case of stock brokers, you broker might be your only access to really great stock options, as brokers always know through others in their field if a new stock is going to be worth the investment.

Disadvantages of Having a Broker

A key disadvantage of having a broker is that you have to pay a commission fee for their services. Even if you do not make any profits, you still have to pay the broker's fee for using their services. Another disadvantage is that they may give you terrible advice because markets can change suddenly. Moreover, there may be situations where you might feel that the broker is acting in their own interests rather than yours.

Whatever the case might be, you need to weigh the pros and cons of a broker before hiring one to help you out, even though, in most cases, it turns out to be a beneficial relationship.

Brokers are very important when it comes to investments. In certain markets, like real estate, the broker is like a gatekeeper as you cannot see any investment properties without a broker. It does not matter if the person who is showing you the property is not a broker, but rather an agent or realtor, as both have to work under a real estate broker. Real estate is one of the few markets where you cannot do anything without a broker.

Insurance brokers are like a bridge between real estate brokers and stock brokers because, depending on the situation, the insurance broker is similar to the other types, mainly the real estate and stock broker. With a mutual insurance fund, the broker is similar to the real estate broker, being the gatekeeper to the mutual company. The investor has to be a policyholder to be involved, and the insurance broker has to assess any potential policyholder to see how much of a premium is going to be based on lifestyle factors of the policyholder. Meanwhile, in insurance stock, the insurance broker is similar to a stockbroker as he or she wants to make sure that not only does the company make a profit, but that their shareholders get their dividends, and the common stock traders make a profit as well.

Stock brokers, both full-service and discount, or better known as online brokers, are trying to make sure you make a profit. Although it is useful for you to check on your stocks and other investments daily, you don't necessarily have to if you invest in certain funds or bonds. However, brokers can make an investor's life easier even if they charge a commission fee, as they can tell you what can give you a profit. Nevertheless, it is up to you to decide if a broker is right for you.

Chapter 7: Basic Investment Strategies

The world of investment, no matter how well it is broken down, can be a very confusing and intimidating thing to navigate. For many, investing is exactly like a religion: everyone who does it has very strong opinions about it, and they might end up getting their beliefs about investment from one of the many schools of thought that come with investing. These three major schools of thought are The Doomsday Preppers, The Gambling Day-Traders, and The Indexers.

The Doomsday Preppers are the ones who are absolutely convinced the financial system will eventually collapse, so their more popular investments are in gold and real estate. The Gambling Day-Traders, however, are the people you usually see in movies. These are the ones with their desks and walls absolutely plastered with televisions and monitor screens, watching the market every single second of the day and clocking how it changes before they make decisions. Then, The Indexers are the people who simply invest in absolutely everything in order to take full advantage of the slow and steady increase that happens in the overall value of the market.

However, alongside these schools of thought, there are hundreds of thousands of individuals who purchase and then sell corporate securities on the NASDAQ regularly and are very successful. The truth of the matter is that a profitable outcome in the stock market is not a result of mere luck but is simply the constant application of a few rules, tips, and principles that are derived from the true-to-life experiences of millions of investors over time.

Do not get confused, a high IQ score is not a requirement for having success in investment. Many successful investors claim that absolutely everyone has the brainpower to follow the basics of the stock market. Peter Lynch, an investor of the Magellan Fund, says that if someone can make it through 5th grade math, then they can make it and be successful in the stock market.

One of the most important things to do before you begin investing in the stock market is to sit down and chart out your long-term financial goals. Why are you considering investing in the stock market? How long would it be until you earn your money back? What is the purpose of the money you make back? These are all questions that need answers before you begin investing. The great thing is that there is no right or wrong answer. This simple charting of long-term goals helps to figure out which types of investments you should take on, the type of risk you can afford to take with your investments, and what types of stock you should invest in. Not only that, but it helps guide you when it comes to figuring out the type of return you need to see on your investment and weighing overall interest rates.

Remember that the growth of your overall portfolio hinges on three factors that are dependent upon one another: the number of years you choose to invest, the amount of capital you invest, and the amount of net annual earnings you will eventually see on your capital.

Another overall tip is to start saving and investing as soon as possible. Save as much as you can in order to receive the absolute highest return that is possible, and always make sure you are evaluating your risk philosophy. If a particular investment someone is trying to convince you to buy goes against this personal philosophy, then it is not worth the stress to go against what you believe is right.

With that risk philosophy comes understanding your risk tolerance. "Risk tolerance" is simply a psychological trait that is rooted within one's DNA. It is something that becomes positively influenced over time by income, education, and wealth, but it can be negatively impacted by age. As someone gets older, risk tolerance has a tendency to decrease, which means that an individual can end up taking unnecessary risks in the market in their old age. Someone's risk tolerance is merely how he or she feels about the risk being taken with his or her money and the degree to which anxiety festers when the risk is present. Every single person varies in terms of this threshold, and there is no right or wrong balance, but this principle is important when determining your own risk philosophy.

The fact that it varies with age means it always needs to be re-evaluated.

Understand that risk tolerance can also be affected by someone's *perception* of risk. For example, someone who has been in and survived an airplane crash will probably view driving a car as safer than flying in an airplane. Studies show that flying in an airplane is massively safer than driving a car, but that individual's experience influenced his or her perception of the risk that comes with a particular situation. This means that as you obtain more knowledge about the stock market and investing in general, it will influence where you invest your money and how difficult it is to liquidate an investment, and it will consistently alter the types of risks you are willing to take with your developing portfolio.

However, assessing your risk tolerance is different from controlling your emotions. The biggest obstacle to any sort of stock market profit is someone's inability to control his or her emotions in order to make logical decisions. In short-term investments, the price of a company's individual stock has a tendency to reflect the combined emotions of the entire investment community of that company. In other words, when the majority of people feel positively about a company, the stock price has a tendency to rise. On the flip side, when the majority of investors in a company are worried about it, the stock prices have a tendency to decline.

For basic terminology purposes, someone who feels negatively about the market is called a "bear," and the positive counterpart is a "bull." During daily stock market exchanges, these short-term movements in stock prices and the selling of stock are usually driven by hopes, rumors, and speculations that are rooted in emotion rather than logic, and the fights between "bears" and "bulls" can heighten anxious emotions. Do *not* fall into this trap. Do *not* let a daily slump in a stock worry you too much. Likewise, do not let a massive high in a stock cause you to have too much faith in the company. The stock market is all about logical moves, not emotional ones.

When first beginning to invest, it is important to learn the basics of the stock market and the securities that comprise the market as a whole. Unless you are purchasing in an exchange traded fund (ETF), your focus needs to be on individual securities rather than on the market as an entire massive entity. There are four main areas you should be educated in before beginning to invest: financial definitions and metrics, stock market order types, the most popular methods for selecting and timing stock, and the different types of investment accounts that are available to you. Know these subjects well before you begin investing.

As Warren Buffett has said, "Risk comes from not knowing what you are doing." Your risk tolerance can be managed by simply knowing what you are getting yourself into.

Another great tip for beginners is to diversify your investments. Many experienced investors will tell every single beginner the same thing: the most popular way to manage all risks while still being able to learn how the market works is to fully and completely diversify one's portfolio. Do not put all your eggs in one basket and then watch what that basket does. This is a risky technique, and one that only experienced investors are able to do and profit from well. If you can diversify your portfolio, it means that one single bad event does not tank your entire portfolio and rob you of what you've invested in the first place.

Not only that, but the diversification of a portfolio allows someone to be able to recover from the loss of a total investment should there be something devastating that happens to the stock market while you are an investor.

Another thing that beginners need to make sure of is that they avoid "leverage." Leverage is nothing other than utilizing borrowed money in order to execute some sort of stock market strategy. If you do not have your own money to execute it, then you do not need to be executing it. In a specific account called a "margin account," brokerage firms and banks can legally loan you money to purchase stocks, usually up to 50% of the purchase value of those stocks. This borrowed money then has to be paid back with the money that you feel you are going to get from the stock market. However, you will find yourself in a massive bind if the stock you thought was going to soar actually plummets.

Stay away from borrowed money.

The stock market takes patience. If you can work it over a long period of time, you will see returns on what you invest. Equity investments, historically, have enjoyed the highest return on money above all other types of investments. Not only that, but they have been proven easy to liquidate, have total visibility, and also have active regulation in order to make sure everyone is playing on an even field. The truth of the matter is that the younger you start, the greater your final result. You just have to make sure that you start walking before you start running. If you do not, you are going to get yourself into a lot of financial trouble.

Understand this: there is no harm in talking to someone who already has knowledge. Talk to someone and find out your options. Set up an appointment with investment advisors at your bank, and ask them questions. Let them help you figure out your goals. Let them be your sounding board. Once you understand all of the different types of accounts, as well as the positive and negatives that come with each account, then you are more educated than you were before, and you are educated enough to begin to make the appropriate decisions for your future.

This is your financial future we are talking about. Do not be afraid to consult a professional. Just do not get yourself into a situation where you are paying exorbitant amounts of money for that professional opinion. There are plenty of people out there who will advise you upfront for free or for a very, very miniscule price.

Once you make the decision to enter the stock market with a set sum of money, the easiest way to get in is to purchase stock from companies you are familiar with and know already. If you are someone who purchases a hot green tea every single day, then buy Starbucks shares. If you are someone who utilizes Apple technology products every single day of your life, then buy stock in Apple. The best way to figure out how to watch and learn the stock market is to do it by utilizing stock you already understand.

Another thing to understand is that you do not need to be worried about taxes. No taxes are due when you sell at a loss. If you try to find ways to navigate around the "tax man," you are going to make poor decisions with your money, and you will end up losing more money than you gain. Would you rather gain $50,000 that you need to pay taxes on, or would you rather waste your time trying to navigate around those taxes, wait too long, and watch the stock plummet into a loss?

Do not put your energy into avoiding taxes. If you are paying taxes on the money, then you are making money, and you are doing it right.

A tip to consider once you become a little more familiar with the stock market is to not buy all of your stocks at once. If you want to maximize your profit, then you need to stage your buys in sections. This allows you to work your orders so that you can get the best price for your stock over time.

Another rule of thumb is to understand the difference between damaged companies and damaged stocks. There are no refunds on Wall Street, but making sure you understand the difference takes time and knowledge.

For example, when Cendant was defrauded by CUC International through a multi-series of incredibly corrupt financial agreements, the stock plummeted. Does that mean that the stock needed to be purchased? No, because the company itself had been damaged. On the flip side, when Eastman Chemical officially announced a 4-point fall in their stocks because of a fixable problem, their stock recovered up 8 points in their next quarter because they were able to fix the issue. The company was not damaged, but its stock temporarily was.

It takes a keen sense of how business works, as well as how an individual business operates, in order to determine whether the company is damaged or whether the stock is damaged. However, once you can figure out the difference, you will be able to accurately discern whether to buy a stock that is plummeting within a company or not.

While this tip might seem like a no-brainer, it does warrant this statement: do your homework in the stock you plan to invest in. Before you purchase any stock, you need to make sure you have researched all aspects of the company, including their company history. This will give you an idea of how the public views the company and how the company is viewed worldwide, and it will provide a history on what their stocks have done in the past in order to give you a movable chart as to what it will do in the future.

Do not invest in stock you are not familiar with.

Another thing to understand is that the research you do on a stock will help you to avoid the temptation to flee with the masses. No one makes any money when they panic and sell prematurely. There will always be a better time to leave the table of the stock in question, and if you do your research, you will be more willing to lean on your own knowledge instead of leaning on the people who are fleeing the company because their stock has temporarily dropped.

One thing that every investor, both seasoned and beginner, aspires to is to find a takeover. Nothing is more exciting than a takeover because it is very financially lucrative. Many people who find themselves in a takeover can earn two decades' worth of moves in one day from any specific takeover. Thus, people go to great lengths to try and make themselves part of one. However, this practice usually includes purchasing many bad stocks in bad companies in the hope of catching just one takeover.

Here is the issue with that premise: bad companies rarely get any sort of substantial bids. The truth of the matter is that companies that get bids are always wonderful companies with a very cheap stock rather than terrible companies with expensive stock.

A good rule of thumb is never to turn your mind's eye – or your financial eye – towards a company with bad fundamentals.

Another good rule of thumb that many beginners do not take into consideration is the fact that diversity does not mean hundreds. Sometimes, it can feel constraining, but even the biggest experts make this mistake. Do not own too many different names of stock. It is hard to keep up with, it is hard to profit from, and you will do more research into the companies themselves instead of taking that time to research how to maximize your profit. Diversifying a portfolio does not mean owning hundreds of different names of stock.

Alan Anderson

Another good rule of thumb that comes from the tip above is to make sure you sell stock in a company the moment you acquire new stock in a company. This is what investment portfolios that are managed by third parties do: they have a set number of stock names they will adhere to, and if they take on one, they get rid of one so the tally on their number of stock names never goes up.

Even though working the market is a logical process, no one can really avoid putting their own emotions into the game. Thus, if you are going to be an emotional person while playing the market, do not play the "should have, could have, would have" game. This is a damaging emotional train of thought, and it is destructive to the positive mindset that is required in order to make sound investment decisions. In fact, this train of thought can actually lead to terrible decisions that have led many investors close to bankruptcy.

Do not play that emotional game.

Storms and corrections within the stock market are like thunderstorms in real life: they happen, you have to prepare for them, and then they eventually correct themselves. When a storm happens, nearly everyone panics every single time, as if it is a new and first-time event. Then, when the market corrects itself, everyone acts as if this is a new phenomenon. They are laughing and high-fiving and hugging, and it never ceases to amaze me how chocked they are that the market stormed and then corrected itself.

The market will always storm and then correct. That is the history of what the stock market does. Do not panic unless you have a founded reason to panic, and do not sell in bulk unless you have a founded reason to sell in bulk.

Never sell your winning stock over your losing stock. This is what this means: in the emotional world of the stock market, many people will hang on to bad stock and sell off their winning stock in order to recoup their losses. People do this for a number of reasons: sometimes, they feel the bad stock will eventually recuperate; sometimes, they have any emotional investment in the company; and sometimes, they feel they have something to prove. However, one thing is for certain: that bad stock that has stayed bad for months is going to continue to stay bad because the only predictor of future behavior is past behavior, especially in the stock market. Do not sell your winning stock in an attempt to subsidize your losses on your losing stock. Instead, sell your losing stock and wait a day. If you still want it back that badly, then simply buy it back.

However, I promise you, you will not want it back.

Given that we are on the topic of emotion, and have been for a little while now, one of the emotions you have to get rid of, no matter what, is hope. This emotion has no founded reason to be in the game of trading stocks, and hope is what loses people a lot of money over a great span of time. The stock market is logical and based on foundational knowledge, not hope.

The world of business is a dynamic and active entity. It is not static; it never has been and never will be. Understand that this will always bring about unexpected shifts within the market, and these unexpected shifts will catch people off-guard, causing them to experience knee-jerk reactions. However, it is these unexpected shifts that require the greatest type of logical focus you can muster.

It is possible to make and lose great sums of money in these unexpected shifts, and keeping as emotionally stable as you can helps to ensure which direction on the graph you end up falling. Do not be one of those people who lose vast sums of money because of panic.

If you are a beginner, it is going to benefit you to keep an eye on high-level executives who are incredibly versed in the world of the stock market. Why? Because they have perfected the game of relinquishing their emotions in order to make sound financial decisions. They do not simply "quit" a specific company for their own personal reasons. Thus, if the chiefs of the stock market are retreating from a company, then something is very, very wrong. These are the only people you should ever take any stock market advice from when it comes to their actions, and you would do well to listen, especially if they are pulling out.

I know we are harping on a lot about the emotional aspect, as emotion can be detrimental in playing the stock market. The market takes a great deal of patience, and that patience can be hindered by frustrated emotions. There are so many people who sell stocks that have real worth prematurely because the stock is not making them any money at that very second. Then, they regret the decision to sell when the stock they originally invested in eventually takes off because of the real worth that company has to offer. Just like the stock market takes sound logical decisions, it also takes patience, and patience requires the setting aside of personal feelings in order to play the long game.

If you are like the hundreds of thousands of Americans who are paying attention to the stock market through what they see on television, then understand this: not everything said on the television can be taken as truth. All of those money marketing television shows usually grasp the first financial professional they can find that is whizzing by them in order to say a few things on television to fill a time slot, and many of those professionals are not vetted for their performance, competency, or success. Understand that much of what they say might be right for *their* particular situation, but that is as far as it goes. Do not take everything you hear on television as truth about the stock market, and make sure you are getting your information from other sources as well.

Another thing you need to make sure you do is not panic about preannouncements. The only thing preannouncements signal is ongoing weaknesses within the stock of a company. What you need to do after hearing a preannouncement is wait for 30 days while paying attention to what the stock does. Then, whatever the stock does will depend upon the action you take: if you want to purchase, wait to see if the stock begins to do any better. If it does, then pull the trigger and purchase. If you are figuring out whether you should sell, then wait and see if the stock does any better. If it does, hang on to it. If it does not, then sell it.

A preannouncement should not cause a knee-jerk reaction; it should just make you pay attention for the next four weeks to see what the stock does before making a decision.

Whenever you do get to a point where you begin paying attention to the promotion machine, it is something you should never underestimate. Why? Because many analysts can put their emotions into the game as well. They can get behind certain stocks and keep them propelled in an upward direction well beyond any sort of reason that is derived from the knowledge and morals of the company. Wall Street hype and the promotion machine are two different things, and the promotion machine should not be underestimated.

Another way to make sure you are thoroughly educated on the stock you are attempting to invest in is to make sure you can always articulate your reasoning to someone else with complete clarity and foundational knowledge. The truth of the matter is that purchasing and selling stock is a very solitary event, and many people do not take into consideration the value of being able to articulate their investments to another human being. Even if you have to stand in the mirror and talk it through to yourself, make sure you can utilize foundational knowledge of the company, the history of the company, and the morals of the company in order to justify why you believe it is a good stock purchase.

There are many people out there who believe that sometimes the overall market is just not doing well, and that is simply not true. There is *always* a bull market. Do not simply settle for something that is in "bear mode" because you feel you are constrained to a specific amount of time or simply too lazy to find it. There is always something doing well somewhere. Period. Taking the time to find it means that you can capitalize on something that not everyone is capitalizing on.

We have talked about a great deal of tips to adhere to once you begin investing, but we have not talked about how you should set the stage for yourself financially before you begin investing. Investing is not something you can simply do as a knee-jerk reaction to the fact that you need money. There is a stage that needs to be set financially that primes you not only for success, but also to bounce back if you have failures.

And in the stock market, you *will* have eventual failures.

So set the stage for sound monetary investments. This means living on a budget, digging yourself out of as much debt as possible, allocating part of your monthly budget to savings, and making sure you can maintain an emergency fund that always has at least two *full* months' worth of expenses in it at all times should something happen. If something happens, and you find yourself completely devoid of all monetary funds, then you have that account you can use to get by with everything you need for two months, which can give you ample time to get your financials in order, especially with the stock market.

Ideally, you should try to save so you have enough for three or four months. However, setting a goal for two months' worth of full expenditures is a good start. This is how you prime yourself for a sound investing future. With something as volatile and ever-changing as the stock market, you do not want your financials to hinge simply on whether or not you do well.

There is also no shame in asking for help when it comes to setting up your first investment account. For people who are brand new to the game, this process can be incredibly overwhelming, and this is when mistakes are made, especially if someone attempts to do it on his or her own. Here is my recommendation: if anyone is unsure about how to open their first investment account, fund that account, or even select a specific fund to use in the first place, then the first step that needs to be taken is to contact a customer service line for a brokerage firm. All these representatives are always happy to answer basic questions and help guide an individual through the process. They are not there to give specific investment advice, but they most certainly can point an individual towards the specific tools he or she will need to help him or her make the best decision for his or her future investment accounts.

For the beginning investor, there is nothing wrong with keeping it simple. You can do things like automate your contributions every month to the account that has been set up. You can find an all-in-one fund with some sort of allocation that is very appropriate for the low-risk tolerance you should be taking in the beginning, and you can even invest in stocks you know are going to do well because of their trends, should you be attempting to do this on your own. However, if you are a beginning investor, you need to have someone you are consulting who is more knowledgeable about this than you are because it is going to help prevent you from making catastrophic mistakes with your hard-earned money.

Implementing some of these tactics means that it is possible for your monthly portfolio management to be hands-off and automatic, which can save you time and minimize the likelihood of mistakes that can be made at the hands of beginners. Then, when you become a little more knowledgeable about what is happening, you can take on more risk and have a more hands-on approach to your own portfolio. However, implementing some of these tactics will help you to have more time to learn about the stock market in general, which will help you maximize profit along down the road.

Always remember: playing the stock market is always more lucrative when played as a long-term game.

Another thing that beginners need to take into consideration is learning where to invest their money. For many beginning investors, they usually only have one investment account. This account, for most corporate workers, is their 401k plan. This means they are less willing to spend time managing and rebalancing their account, and they are more willing to pick a target-date fund so they can set it and forget it, so to speak.

This tactic works just fine for beginners, and it can be very lucrative in the long run. During this "set it and forget it time," however, the beginning investor should focus on learning how to expand his or her marketable skills so he or she can contribute more to the fund. Many companies usually have a "matching rule" when it comes to a 401K plan, which means they will match your paycheck contribution up to a certain percentage of your paycheck. For someone who is utilizing something like this as his or her only investment account, he or she needs to aim to put back the highest percentage of that matching offer the company has in order to maximize his or her profit in the long run.

It is a very good lesson in budgeting so you can maximize future profit.

Another disciplined approach that can help investment beginners is utilizing the dollar-cost averaging strategy. This is essentially a practice of regularly transferring a very specific amount of money every month into a particular investment account so that funds and stocks can be bought. This means the investor is forced to purchase either more shares at lower prices or fewer shares when the prices are higher. What this does is it regulates the risk the beginning investor is putting into the market, and it enables him or her to continue to invest evenly without sucking his or her own personal budget dry. Just like gambling, skydiving, or any other risk-taking activity can be addictive, the stock market can become just as addictive, especially when the individual has his or her first lucrative "score."

This disciplined practice helps someone foster and develop a healthy relationship with the stock market instead of an unhealthy one.

Another tip for beginners who might be trying to figure out whether they are going to invest is to simply keep investment transactions small. There is no need to wait until you have developed a massive "cash stash" before you can invest. It is possible to purchase a low minimum mutual fund, set up automatic purchases, and/or simply invest random amounts of money whenever you have the extra money to invest. There are many different investment firms and accounts that have low initial deposit setups of $100.00 and then take investment deposits as low as $1.00. Take advantage of these, because it is never too soon to begin investing.

So many beginning investors attempt to find the best way possible to constantly keep track of the market. Some may make the mistake of living their investment lives by their television screen. Others attempt to navigate the fields by riding on the advice of other friends who claim to be "experts" in investing.

Well, there is an avenue that is dependable, and that is the idea of utilizing social data in order to score your main investment ideas. The idea is essentially this: if you see a popular product and understand how the public is reacting to that product or company, you can utilize the positive upswing to recommend a possible investment you should further study up on. For example, fidget spinners have become all the rage, so doing some research into the popular public opinion on these companies is worth a shot when it comes to investing in them.

You can utilize this method in order to gather data as a springboard into conventional research methods for stocks. One example of this is what happened to police officers. A couple of years ago, when it became popular media to broadcast shootings that involved police officers, people took to their social media accounts in order to proclaim, among many other things, that police officers should be utilizing more reliable chest cameras. Pretty soon, there was a skyrocket in the number of chest camera purchases that departments were making, which had a positive impact on the receiving company's stocks.

If you can educate yourself on these types of social markets and quickly deduce decisions when studying up on the company's financials and moral practices, you can really find some serious monetary gains through these transactions.

However, for many, even the minimal-cost stock trading portfolios are a little steep. If you are among the thousands of people who wish to get into the stock market trading sector but do not have the stomach to spend even the small costs that come with low-cost index funds that diversify portfolios, try utilizing something like Robinhood.

Robinhood is a free investment app for a smartphone or tablet that enables someone to invest in the individual stock market. What this means is that Robinhood charges nothing for stock trading, and it means you can invest in singular, individual stocks. This means no upfront costs, no low-maintenance fees for keeping up with a portfolio, and no percentage payout if your stocks end up making you monetary gains.

Just keep in mind that investing in this type of individual stock exchange is riskier than investing in a low-cost index fund portfolio that is diversified.

Another thing to keep in mind annually is to find time to rebalance your investment portfolio. What this means is that you set an asset allocation that most likely reflects your current risk tolerance, as well as your risk capacity. Remember when we talked about how risk tolerance can change with age? This is why portfolios need to be kept up with and checked. You can change your asset allocation and risk tolerance as necessary, which can leave you with a strategy that enables small increases in return while removing yourself from any unnecessary volatility.

However, one of the most important things to keep in mind is not to time the stock market. Do not attempt to play this sort of professional game, where you keep your eyes on technical charts, and you attempt to figure out the stock market in one two-hour sitting. If you are a beginner, do not be afraid to play the beginner game. This game includes picking investments in companies you already understand to have a great public reputation with great products that you know will be around for many more years to come. Do not attempt to try and squeeze every single percentage of return out of the stock of a company that is relatively unheard of. That is a professional investor's game, and you will find that many beginners do not succeed in that game for one reason and one reason only: they simply do not have the experience to do it.

What you need to make sure of is that you understand the company you are investing in. Do your research, read your materials, and understand that you are playing a very popular game with your own money. These types of markets are way too volatile for short-term money, and this is the reason why many professional investors advise beginners to only play the stock market for the long game. Do not pick different stocks simply because you have to diversify, but pick stocks you know will be around within the next five to seven years.

If you are lost with all these tips and are becoming fatigued and bombarded, then you are not alone. Many who are in the beginning stages of merely wanting to invest can become so overwhelmed with information that they give up their research in favor of not making their head spin. If you are reading this book, I suggest you take some time to digest the information already thrown at you. Set the book down, make a checklist of all the things you deem important and necessary, and set it somewhere to study. This book is a wonderful reference tool for all things stock market-related, but it can also be the biggest chunk of ice you have ever bitten off to try and chew.

And that is fine.

However, when you come back, you come back to the first investment every single beginner should make: an index fund that tracks the Standard & Poor's 500 index. It is called an S&P 500 Index Fund, and it single-handedly tracks 500 of the absolute largest stocks that are traded on the New York Stock Exchange and the NASDAQ daily. They are large, they are stable, and they are the billboard epitome of the cross-section of the United States economy. By investing in this instead of simply taking on the entire stock market, it is possible for a beginner to decrease the volatility of money loss substantially while gaining peace of mind that the stocks he or she has invested in are the best in the market.

This is the best type of long-term investment that a beginner should make. The great Warren Buffett has some wonderful advice for those wanting to pick-and-choose their own stocks: an individual should never purchase a stock if he or she is not comfortable holding on to it should the market shut down completely for an entire decade.

It has been proven that an S&P 500 Index Fund will give an individual very strong returns that are equal to (and, sometimes, even greater than) many funds that are managed actively by outside parties. Not only that, but the risk for this type of index fund is minimal compared to other actively managed funds and portfolios. If you combine the incredibly low expense ratios and the low risk capacity, as well as take into account the fact that the beginning investor will not ever have to pick-and-choose their individual stocks, you can easily see how many professional and seasoned investors recommend this exact index fund for beginners.

Now, take a deep breath, and digest what you have just learned. Write all of it down somewhere so you can keep track of the important things you need to understand. Many of these tips come into play before one actually invests, and some of them come into play once an individual has already invested.

However, once you have gathered enough knowledge and experience with the stock market, it is time to progress to tips and tricks built for those with a more intermediate knowledge of how the stock market works.

Just understand this: no matter the type of education you have behind you when it comes to the stock market, it never hurts to refresh the basics.

Chapter 8: Intermediate Investment Strategies

Once you have some experience with investing under your belt, you are ready to tackle some more involved tips when it comes to working the stock market to your advantage. Understand that these tips build off the basics we talked about in the previous chapter and should not be tackled until you have mastered the previous chapters. For some people, it only takes a few months. However, for many people, it can take years to master the basics of the stock market.

However, once you get there, these tips are for you.

Choosing your investment platform is necessary, especially if your first move was to invest in the S&P 500 Index Fund. For many investors who have spent some time with the stock market, they wish to branch out from this type of beginner's fund. That is fine and highly encouraged, but you have to make sure you understand the platforms out there for you to utilize.

Using online stock brokers is one platform, and they are essentially brokers that are available online. You can do everything you need without ever having to speak to a person on the phone, which is nice for many people who enjoy running their lives online. These types of brokers are often much cheaper than a traditional brick-and-mortar broker, which requires the booking of an appointment to go meet with an expert face to face.

Then, there is a financial advisor. Some people choose to invest with a specific financial advisor because they enjoy this face-to-face interaction along with the professional advice that comes with it. However, be prepared to pay a premium price for premium service. Usually, people who have large sums of money to invest hand it over to a face-to-face financial advisor so they do not have to do any of the work. With an online broker, there is still a level of work the investor has to do, and it can make investing larger sums of money nerve-wracking because you never do see the face of whoever is handling your money.

However, many people are more than willing to pay a premium fee for the premium service of handing over their money to a person they have grown to trust in order to stay hands-off with their investments.

Then, there are robo-advisors. These are online brokers, like Wealthfront and Betterment, which offer the specific benefits of a financial advisor with the ease of use that comes with utilizing an online broker. These robo-advisors are growing in popularity, and they remove a lot of the stress that comes with having to understand when and how to invest. It takes away the anxiety of meeting someone in person, and many of these applications instantly diversify someone's portfolio in several different stocks and bonds.

Not only that, but many of these services also offer automatic allocations that will adjust based on goals, and they prompt the investor to reset at a particular point in time.

However, do not confuse robo-advisors with investment applications. Investment applications do have automated tendencies, as well as take on the ability to not have to talk to anyone in person, but they also eliminate the need for research. These types of applications, like Stash, also allow people to invest as little as $5 right from their phone and have a minimum startup investment that ranges anywhere between $5 and $50. These are growing in popularity, not simply because of their ease of use, but also because people can easily invest and keep track of their investments right from their smartphone or tablet.

However, if it makes you nervous to utilize any of these cyber investment strategies, there are also specific funds and programs that you can utilize. Not only that, but there are plenty of funds you can use where you can meet face to face with a person while cutting down the costs of investing and still having additional benefits tacked on to your diversified investment portfolio.

First off, there are direct mutual fund accounts. If you want to avoid paying broker fees, you can utilize this type of account to purchase mutual funds directly from most mutual fund companies. Not only are these types of mutual funds a smart investment decision in their own right, but they also house the concept of avoiding additional fees being written into them in order to cut down on the overall cost of investing for an individual.

Then, there is a DRIP, or dividend reinvestment program. This is another wonderful way for someone, as an investor, to avoid paying all of those brokerage fees by purchasing a stock directly from the specified company. This is not a common practice with all companies, so there might be a company you want to invest in that will not allow this practice, but many larger companies offer it. Sometimes, they will even offer discounts and incentives to the investor directly if the individual sets up recurring investments or purchases larger blocks of stock from them.

Alan Anderson

As a beginner, many will recommend staying with mutual funds or ETFs by utilizing a direct mutual fund account or an online broker. However, once you become more familiar with the stock market and how it works, all of the options mentioned above become available to you. If you are someone who prefers ease of use over meeting face to face with someone, applications like Betterment offer an incredibly simple way to gain exposure to the stock and bond market without much upfront research. You essentially deposit money into the account like a savings account, choose your risk tolerance on a scale of 1 to 10, and then the application invests in the overall market for you.

However, once you choose the type of investment account you want to utilize, the next step is figuring out the type of monetary purpose that the investment account is going to be used for. For many beginners, they simply invest and hope for the best. There is no outline for where that money is going to go other than they know there was money to be made. As an investor with experience, you need to make sure you understand how important it is to your investing capabilities to have a purpose for the money you are investing and making.

However, regardless of the purpose for the money, there are only two types of accounts you can utilize: a general taxable account or an IRA (individual retirement account).

The great thing about an IRA is that it provides certain tax advantages as an incentive to save for one's retirement. The downside to an IRA is that there are imposed lawful limits on how much you can contribute to the account each year and when you can begin to withdraw from it. Within the world of IRAs, there are three you need to be familiar with that are suggested the most by professionals.

For starters, there is a traditional IRA, which is where your contributions might qualify for a deduction on your tax return. In addition to that perk, there is the potential that the earnings you make from this account can grow in a tax-deferred setting until the time you need to withdraw it at your retirement age. The primary argument that convinces people to go with this traditional IRA account is that most people feel they will be in a lower tax bracket when they retire. Thus, paying taxes on this money at any point in time will be cheaper than paying them when they are earned.

Then, there is a Roth IRA. In a Roth IRA, your contributions made to the account are after tax, and the money that grows from it can grow tax-free while you save. The massive benefit to this type of account is that withdrawals at the time of retirement are completely tax-free. However, you have to meet specific requirement conditions in order for that to happen. This is the number one IRA account recommended to people by investment professionals, and those tax-free benefits are the reason why.

The last one is a Rollover IRA. This is a specific account that is created by rolling over one account into another, such as a company-sponsored 401(k). For example, if you have a 401(k) with a specific employer that you intend to leave, you can create a Rollover IRA that rolls this money over into a new IRA account created for the 401(k) benefits your new company is going to offer. This makes job transitions much easier on people while minimizing monetary risk and avoiding early withdrawal fees in order to transfer bulk sums of money.

The bottom line is that these IRAs provide a great deal of monetary support and security for future monetary assets. There are tax-free perks that come for those who qualify; general taxable investment accounts are not going to give you this type of security. However, an IRA is not the only way you can save for retirement. An IRA is simply what has been created to make sure that saving for retirement is amplified and secured to its fullest extent.

However, the truth of the matter is that if your purpose for investing is anything other than retirement, like buying a home or beginning a business, a regular brokerage account is going to serve you just fine. Keep in mind that the money you earn when you sell security for more than you paid for it, which is called your capital gains, is taxable off the top alongside the dividends you receive. As long as you keep that in mind, you will be able to choose the best general taxable account for whatever purpose your money is going to serve, if it is not for retirement.

Now comes the part where you need to select your individual investments. The great thing about being an intermediate player with a secured foundation in the basics is the fact that you will be able to knowledgeably select your own investments versus trusting an individual or an electronic system with who they invest in for you.

However, it can get a little overwhelming, so we are going to break this down in the best way we can.

If you end up deciding that you want to venture into the market and purchase your own individual stocks, you have to make sure you take the slow and steady approach. Just because you have been playing the stock market for a few months, or even a few years, does not make you an expert in all of the companies playing on the field. A general rule of thumb that everyone needs to abide by is to not put more than 10% of your own individual portfolio into individual stocks you choose until you become comfortable with what you are doing.

One of the most important factors in being a successful investor is not simply the stocks and funds you choose. Successful investing also depends on choosing the proper asset allocation, which refers to the overall mix of cash, bonds, and stocks you hold in your (hopefully) diversified portfolio. Not only that, but making sure you stick with your investment plan will also help you to make logical and sound decisions while steering you away from emotionally charged ones. Many people make emotionally fueled decisions when they see stock they have invested in take a massive dip. Keeping in tune with your investment plan, or even having an investment plan from the beginning, will help you to determine whether that plummet in stock price is simply the market regularly fluctuating or whether that is something you really do need to get out of.

Being able to take your emotions out of the picture will enable you to be more proactive with your money. Instead of simply wondering where your money went, tell your money what to do. For many, they know what needs to be done with their money, and they simply do not want to do it. Secure a budget, get rid of all of the debt you can, save, and allocate a monthly expenditure that you put towards your investments.

It sounds like a beginner's tip, but you would be surprised at how many people have been playing the stock market for years and end up losing everything they have ever made because they do not want to follow those four basic rules.

One of the biggest things you need to look for when investing in your own individual stock is the risk versus reward factor. Creating a tax-efficient portfolio and diversifying your assets in order to work for your benefit means making sure the reward outweighs the risk. If there is a higher chance of risk, what that means is that there is a higher chance of you losing the principal balance of the money you invested in the first place. However, if there is a displacement of reward to risk, then you stand a better chance of making money you can keep over the long-run.

Playing the stock market for a few months, or a few years, does not suddenly mean you can make risky investments in order to double, or even triple, your assets. It simply means you are at a point where you can better evaluate individual companies and make decisions on your own about whether to invest in them or not.

And those decisions will be based on in-depth research.

If you are going to go the route of having an in-person financial advisor, do not be afraid to ask for better rates. In order to keep as much of your up-front capital as possible, learn to negotiate. All it takes is a little guts and the ability to simply ask. The only thing that you have to lose is a little bit of time, and if you are working on a budget, you can use this idea of asking for better rates in anything. Whether it is your cable, internet, or phone bill, if there are deals and better rates out there you can secure, that is more money you can put towards your overall investments.

Another thing you will be able to do as an investor who has spent some time in the stock market is to have more confidence when it comes to automating your assets. Usually, many investment portfolios will be able to link themselves up to your bank account so you can automatically deposit money into them. Many beginners automate this process simply because they do not want to think about their investments. People who have been playing the stock market for a while are able to automate this process because they have thought about their investments, and they know that they are making the right moves that accumulate the most money overtime.

The difference between the two is simply the attention to long-term financial goals.

For beginners, we outlined the S&P 500 Index Fund. However, there are also many other index funds that people who have been playing the stock market for a while can invest in: there is a small company index, a midsize company index, an emerging market index, a government bond index, an international index, and the list goes on and on. If you are someone who enjoyed the S&P 500 Index Fund, but you still want to diversify your portfolio further, then you can continue to tack on these index funds to your portfolio and hold little pieces of many companies that will accumulate money for you over the long run with your investments. This is a wonderful option if you do not want to take the time to research all of your companies and build your own portfolio.

Regardless of the time you have spent in the stock market game, diversification is key, no matter your age or risk tolerance.

If you are going to go the way of index funds, here is what it should cost you: an index fund should cost as little as .09% to .30%, and even though this might seem like a tiny difference, over time, this can make a massive difference in how much money you have for your future monetary goals.

The truth of the matter is that the best way to maximize any investment or savings plan you decide to utilize for the stock market is to put the monthly deposits on autopilot. Whether you set it up with your company to withdraw it from your paycheck before you see it, or whether you set an automatic deposit that happens every single month, the less you think about it, the greater chance you have of not backing out of a monthly deposit because of some asinine reason.

If you can put your monthly deposit into your investment and/or savings account on autopilot, then do it.

However, one thing that does need mentioning here that was mentioned in the beginners' chapter is to not forget your estate plan. Financial planning has a great deal of focus in emergency planning, and many people will suggest that keeping a savings account you do not touch that houses six months' worth of bills is necessary. However, what happens in the event of premature death? Will you end up having enough assets to financially take care of the people you leave behind? While that sounds like an emergency question, it actually is not. It is a question of your estate.

In order to make sure you have an estate plan, one of the basic things you need to outline is a will. Within that will, you need to have clear and distinct details as to your monetary plan, your personal savings, your employee benefits, and even your life insurance. You need to make sure these funds are allocated properly to members of your family so that they are taken care of after you are gone. Life happens, and if you focus solely on preparing for the emergencies, you will miss out on what is actually important when it comes to your financial plan.

Do not forget your estate plan.

Another thing to strive to is being the owner of capital. The truth of the matter is that appreciation is never actually taxable until you decide to be taxed. This means that, up until that taxation point, you have complete control. However, not only do you have control, but those gains you see are usually taxed at long-term capital gains tax rates. Simply put, if there is ever a point where you can be compensated with stock rather than ordinary income, there will always be a greater long-term advantage for you monetarily.

Sometimes, it is not simply about how much you get paid, but about how you get paid in the first place.

In the beginners' chapter, we also talked about how important it was to get out of debt. However, we did not address how important it is to manage debt in order to stay out of it. For many people who dig themselves into debt, it is hard to escape because they continue to accrue debt. Some college-age students make the mistake of opening their first credit card in order to supplement their lifestyle until they can get a better job, and they continue to utilize that credit card while only paying the minimum balance, which digs them into larger amounts of debt in the long run.

Debt management is all about finding a way to strategically pay down your most expensive debt first, whether that debt is credit card debt, student loan debt, or housing debt. However, this type of monetary management is also about avoiding future debt and looking at areas where you can cut back spending and even spend smarter. For example, if you find yourself purchasing coffee every morning or eating out at lunch and putting it on a credit card, consider cutting back those purchases by making your own coffee and taking your own lunch until you get to a point financially where you do not have to put those small purchases on a credit card.

This will save you ample amounts of money in the long run, which will give you more money to invest for your future.

Alan Anderson

When managing your debt, it is also important to look at the ideas of refinancing. Every chart that came out for the year 2017 predicted that interest rates would continue to rise, and that is exactly what happened. If you find yourself in a place where you are still attempting to pay off debt while trying to save for your future, consider consolidating your loans and refinancing them somewhere with a lower interest rate. The downside to this is that many of these refinancing institutions will "start over" your payment cycle. What this means is that if you took out the loan under the assumption that it was going to take six years to pay down, and you paid down two years before refinancing, the refinancing process will usually put you back at the beginning of those six year payments, unless you personally suggest otherwise.

However, if you can put $200 back into your pocket every month by refinancing, that is more money that you have to invest with and financially plan for. Not only that, but refinancing at a locked-in lower interest rate can save you money over the course of the years you have to pay down this debt while fluctuating interest rates continue to rise.

If you are one of many individuals who work for a corporate entity, then look into their possible options for flexible spending accounts. If your company offers them, take full advantage of them. For many of these FSAs, the employer usually offers out-of-pocket medical expenses and care cost contributions that match what you put in, kind of like a 401(k) that invests in your health. The tax savings on this is substantial because money that is deferred into these FSAs avoids all taxes. Not only that, but you can save yourself thousands of dollars a year by maximizing your own personal FSA contributions and writing them off come tax time.

Just remember, with these types of accounts, there is a use-it-or-lose-it stipulation. Simply put, unused money by the end of the year is forfeited, so make sure you accurately estimate your contributions.

When it comes to investing, it is important to understand why you are investing because the risk management strategy is different for every investment you make. Retirement income planning, and the risk tolerance that comes along with it, is different from a simple savings account or wanting to accumulate wealth in a diversified index fund portfolio. The risk versus reward factor is different, and the way you will go about setting up your accounts for the long-term is also different. The rules of investment are applied differently, depending on the purpose of your money, and it is wise to always be aware of these different rules, and make sure they are being applied correctly to the account you are utilizing.

Never underestimate the power of compound interest. There are many people who have chosen to work low- to mid-salary careers and have worked how to grow wealthy into their budget. If you can learn how to manage and invest your money, then compound interest will do the rest over time. Start by trying to invest $100 a month. Then, add that money every single month to your investments, no matter what. Between keeping your portfolio costs low and diversifying your assets, it is possible to get yourself financially free.

How is this possible? Well, it is simply the power of compound interest.

How does compound interest work? Compound interest is simply interest paid on the initial principal you deposit, as well as the accumulated interest on the money you have invested. In this glorious theory, it is like a double chocolate topping.

Alan Anderson

What happens is this: you earn interest on the money you initially deposit, and you *also* earn money on the interest you have already earned, so you are earning interest on the interest.

This means that if you were to invest $10,000.00 at 5% interest, you would earn a total of $512. Adding it all up at the end of the year, your account would have $10,512. The next year, at the same 5%, it would be calculated not on the $10,000, but on the $10,512. Thus, the next year's 5% that you would earn would be$ 538.

Go with compound interest. Always.

If you choose to take the route of automatically depositing money into your savings account, you have to make sure you stay on top of your money. If you are going to utilize a financial advisor, then you have to stay in contact with them. There are plenty of people who end up being assigned a financial advisor, but then they become stuck, losing all of their gains when their financial advisor either leaves the company or is laid off, and their portfolio is not transferred to someone else. If you are using a financial advisor, make sure you hear from him or her at least twice a month. If you are staying on top of your investments yourself, it is wise to check them at least twice a week.

No one is going to value your money as much as you do. Do not completely entrust someone to do what is best with your money and then back off all together. You have to stay on top of things if you are going to bring in a third-party candidate to manage your money.

Do not be afraid to take risks with your money when you are younger. Why? Because if you hit a financial snag where you see more losses than you would have wished, you have more available time to make up those losses by using long-term investment moves. If you have ever taken a course on derivatives, then you have learned about the gambling aspect of the stock market. You have learned that it can lead to some very incredible gains, but also some very stark losses. If you find yourself taking these risks and they do not pay off, the fact that you have invested younger means you have more time to recoup that lost money without making a dent in your long-term financial goals.

Just make sure to invest only with the money you have.

Another thing to keep in mind is to always take advantage of free money. If your company offers a match point for 401k, then put in the largest percentage of your paycheck in order to have the largest percentage of free money the company will give you. The same goes for FSAs and any other accounts you will come across that can be beneficial to you that offer free – or matching – money.

Investing can also help you save on taxes. If you can invest in tax-saving mutual funds, then it will allow you to learn more about many of the different investment vehicles available to you, and you can expand your investment portfolio to include equity-based mutual funds. In the long run, this can put more of your money back into your pocket because not all of it is subjected to taxation.

There are many investment accounts and portfolios out there that will not tax you on the money that is in the account or on the money you have put into the account. This can be incredibly beneficial when lowering your overall taxable income, so make sure you do your research and know where to find them.

The younger you can start investing, the better off you are going to be in the long run. However, the more you can invest early on, the more financial benefits you can reap in the short term. If you can invest more of your paycheck early on in your career and early on in your lifetime, it not only sets you up for better long-term financials, but it also provides a growing cushion that you can tap into earlier on if a life emergency happens.

Obviously, the best scenario is to not touch it at all, but life happens. Invest while you are young, and invest as much as you can while you are young, and it will give you greater returns not only in the long run, but in the short run as well.

Educating yourself about the stock market and investing responsibly knows no boundaries or experience level. Always be educating yourself, always do your research, always make sure your money has a purpose, and always make sure you know where it is being invested. Blind investments will *always* come back to bite you. The more educated you are, the less of a risk the stock market is, regardless of the type of risk tolerance and risk capacity you have for your portfolio.

Investing also helps you to prepare for life after debt. In this day and age, over 80% of the United States population is in some sort of debt, and the average time it takes to pay off $30,000 worth of student loans is 12.3 years. Thus, many are focused on paying off their debt and not focused on the life they will lead after their debt is paid off. This is why making a budget and allocating funds into an investment portfolio despite the debt you are paying off is essential. I know it is hard to believe right now, but you *will* have a life after debt.

And you are going to want that life to be financially sound.

This means that an investment schedule is more important than ever. When you have more money going out to places than what you have coming in, you have to stay on top of where that money is going at any given moment. Stick to a recurring investment schedule, and make sure to set times in your week to check up on your investments. Pretty soon, the practice will become a mindless task, and it will not be as taxing on you emotionally and mentally.

One of the greatest things you can do for your financial existence is to invest in dividend-paying companies. This is the concept of being paid in order to hold shares within a company, and it gives someone a regular flow of passive income. Some companies reward their shareholders with monthly dividend checks simply by being stockholders in the company. AT&T, Chevron, General Motors, and Pfizer are just a few of the companies that pay monthly dividends to those who hold stock in their company.

Take advantage of and invest in as many of these companies as you can realistically afford to invest in. It is a wonderful way to build a monthly passive income without ever actually having to go to work for someone.

However, even with all of these tips, it can be hard to look at those who have made their fortune in investing and think it impossible to make a bad move. After all, with the likes of Warren Buffett running around, should you not be taking risky investments that will pay off in the long run? Here is the difference between you and Warren Buffett: you are investing in companies, whereas Warren Buffett is buying them.

Alan Anderson

However, hearing from the experts on the basic tips they still follow to this day can help you sift through all this information and pinpoint what is really going to help you in the long run right now, regardless of the type of investments you have.

With all of the information thrown at you in this book, the one thing you can always rely on is the advice of those who have proven these models to work.

Chapter 9: Tips For Investing From The Experts

Housed in this chapter are tips from experts in all areas of the investment field. They are going to give us the foundational truth they always keep at the back of their minds when it comes to investing their own money or managing others' money. When you find yourself at a loss and completely overwhelmed with the information out there on the stock market, always come back to this chapter.

It will help you sift through all the advice, all the voices, and all the analyst-based talking points so you can make the best decision for you and your personal investments.

Greg Collette, former CEO of Deutsche Bank's commodity ETF business, says that for each investment you make, you have got to understand the risks you are taking. Do not expect your financial advisor to do this research for you. If you are not willing to do this work yourself, you just need to keep your money safely in a bank.

Dave Ramsey, author of *The Total Money Makeover* and one of the most popular individuals for helping people climb out of debt, says you have got to walk to the beat of a very different drummer as compared to everyone else in your circle of friends. The beat the wealthy are marching to is the one you need to be listening out for. The goal for your personal investments is not to be normal, because normal, in this day and age, is broke. Listening to your friend is only going to get you where your friend is. If you want to be where an expert is,

Alan Anderson

then listen to the expert.

Warren Buffett, the infamous American business magnate, gives us exactly what we need to become rich: he says you need to be afraid when others around you are greedy, and be greedy when others around you are afraid. What he means is this: stock trends are not always the safest investments. Just because everyone around you is lurching for a particular stock does not mean they are making a conscious decision based on logic and reason. Many of the knee-jerk reactions seen on the market within the halls of Wall Street are based solely on emotion and not much on knowledge.

What Buffett is telling us is to do the research before investing and not to pay attention to what others are doing around us.

Clark Kendall, who is the president and founder of Kendall Capital Investment, says the most common mistake people make with their retirement planning is not diversifying their investment strategy. To him, there is absolutely no reason he has found as to why an individual cannot diversify his or her risk when it comes to the stock market.

In other words, you do not have to use the same risk tolerance for every single investment you make. Just as you need to diversify the investment in your portfolio, you can also diversify the risks within every individual investment in your portfolio.

Suze Orman, who is an infamous American author and motivational speaker, simply says that no one has ever achieved any sort of security by being weak, scared, and/or afraid. To her, confidence is contagious and will give you the fuel you need in order to succeed at the stock market. How do you gain that confidence? Continue to educate yourself on the stock market and the investments you make.

Jeanne Kelly, who is a credit coach, says that you need to make sure you stay on top of your credit report. Check for errors, and check it as often as you can without it actually affecting your score. One simple mistake on your credit score can cost you a great deal of money, and if you are not actively looking at your credit report in order to protect it against specific errors, then understand that no one else is doing it for you, either. Take 15 minutes twice a year to check it and go through it with a fine-toothed comb.

Mark Wingo, the author of *Wingonomics*, says that you should run your household like it is a business, and manage your finances like it is a bank. He says the lack of money many households experience is not a problem or mismanagement of life; it is a problem and mismanagement of organization and budget. He does not want to see this type of mismanagement hold people back from maximizing their premium earning potential. Get your budget and monetary expenditure under control, and make sure you are not living beyond your means.

Gyutae Park, who is a co-owner of Money Crashers Personal Finance, says that in order to have a secure and successful financial future, it is important to make sure an individual adopts the mindset of spending after saving. If you make sure to set aside funds for the future each pay cycle you obtain, then this is the way to ensure you will have plenty of money regardless of the investment or retirement account you choose. This bases itself, in part, off the idea of automating your finances – making sure you work savings into your budget will ensure a sound financial future.

Renee Rifkin, who is an Australian entrepreneur and stockbroker, says there is one simple question you should ask yourself when purchasing stock: Would you buy the whole company? If you would not purchase the company, do not purchase their stock.

Catherine Garrison, who is a senior financial advisor from Moss Adams Wealth Advisors, says you should set aside some time twice a month in order to update your budget and check your account to make sure they are balancing themselves out. In this day and age where plastic is used more than money, it is very easy for spending to get out of control because there is no longer that tangible aspect to money. It is merely digital. It is much easier to keep one's spending under control if you set aside time in your schedule to check things, rebalance things, and make sure you are not going over your budget.

Robert Kiyosaki, who is an American investor and self-help author, says it is not about how much money you bring in, but it is about how much money you keep. Not only that, but it is also about how hard your money works for you and how many generations you plan to keep this money for. In other words, making money is not the only priority in the stock market. If it is your only priority, then you have not planned your financial future very well, and you need to go back to the drawing board.

Sir John Templeton, who is an American-born British stock investor and businessman, gives us the four most dangerous words in the world of investing: "this time it's different." Trust the expert, it is *never* different.

Vicki Robin, who is the co-author of *Your Money or Your Life*, simply says that how you spend your money on a daily basis is how you vote on what exists in our culture. What she is trying to point out is the societal responsibility we have when it comes to investing in the stock market. Simply put: if you want something to exist in the future, then you need to invest in it. This should not be something that is lived by when it comes to making money on investments, but it does help you keep a moral compass when it comes to who you invest in.

Todd Tressider, a financial coach at Financialmentor.com, gives us a different take on risk management. He talks about the simple mathematical truth that is worked into how many compounds are needed to create wealth and how it will help someone mitigate his or her risk management. For example, a 10% loss only requires a 15% gain to get back to an even keel, but if you experience a 40% loss, it is going to require an outstanding 95% gain in order to get back to a break-even point. In his mind, the math is undeniable: it is simply not about how much you make when you are right; it is also about how much you lose when you are wrong.

Jeff Rose, the founder of Good Financial Cents, says that you need to be hesitant with friendly advice. He also subscribes to the mentality that if you want to be where the experts are, then you need to follow the experts. If you listen to a family member, a friend, or a close coworker, then their advice is only going to get you where they are. Instead of attempting to seek approval on a random stock tip or piece of advice, simply do the research yourself. Taking responsibility for your losses is just as important as taking responsibility for your gains. Be hesitant with the friendly advice, and always ask questions.

Jaime Tardy, who has interviewed over 100 millionaires EventualMillionaire.com, says you should find an investing mentor. She recommends finding someone who is doing specifically what you are doing and, even if they seem untouchable, find a way to reach out to them. Warren Buffett had a mentor, and Bill Gates had a mentor, and if the two richest human beings on this planet had mentors, then it means it is a good tip for you to abide by. A mentor can teach you about what happens in real life and not merely spout off shiny tips and facts regarding things and concepts taught in classrooms and written in books.

Alexander Dolan, the founder of Fully Alive Life Coaching, tells us to follow the 20% rule. Essentially, what this means is that after you have done the research into the stock market and purchased your first stock, you need to keep an eye on it. Once it has either gained or lost 20% of its purchase value, then it is time to sell and move on to the next option. An overall rule is that if a particular stock stays above 20% or higher for more than three consecutive weeks, then you can hold onto it for up to eight weeks. However, the goal is to sell while you are still ahead, and it is always an option to buy back the stock again after it falls, thereby making more money from it.

Tyler Gray, a financial advisor at SageOak Financial, tells us you cannot beat the market. His biggest investment "secret" is that you simply cannot outsmart the stock market in any way you implement, and research backs him up on this statement. Instead of attempting to do massive amounts of research in order to find the next hot deal or stock, he says that many investors are simply better off owning a global, diversified portfolio at a low cost with passively managed mutual funds.

John Paul Engel, who is the president of Knowledge Capital Consulting, has a tip for us that is based on Gray's advice: invest in solid companies. Investing in a company that is out of favor with the public, even though they have significant assets, is not a good investment. However, there are also assets a company can hold that might not always be reflected in their stock price. For example, if a company owns a lot of real estate or has a lot of patents, then that is a solid company despite the fact that their stock price might be low or not fluctuating the way you might like. He says that looking for solid companies to invest in is not just about public image and dividends; it is also about the type of ownership the company itself has.

He also states that you need to take a look at the management of a company: if the management of the company has a good track record, then it will be a good investment. However, if the current company's management does not have a good track record, then it is not a solid investment.

Shanna Tingum, a financial advisor Edward Jones, tells us to simply implement imperfectly. What she means is that getting started with as much as you can afford as soon as you can does not require all of the upfront knowledge like many claim. She says you should begin automatically investing on a monthly basis into some sort of mutual fund while you are doing your research, and then you can reallocate and move as necessary whenever you begin to learn more about the market and about specific funds and accounts you can open. She states that getting started is exactly half the battle and that it is possible in this day and age to get started without having a perfect knowledge-base on how the stock market works.

Sam Seiden, who is the Chief Education Officer for Online Trading Academy, tells us to keep our eye on the US dollar. One way to figure out whether the economy is doing well, he says, is to take a look at the inflation and deflation of the US dollar as compared to the global market. This is what will tell an individual exactly how well the US economy and its markets are performing, and it can help guide investment decisions.

Then, there is advice from the mysterious Spencer, who is the founder of MilitaryMoneyManual.com. He says to always maximize any tax-free earnings available to you. While his advice and website targets military individuals who want to invest, this rule of thumb goes for any individual who finds him or herself with a sum of tax-free money: invest it in a tax-free account. He wants to make sure that everyone maximizes their tax-free pay, should they ever receive it. Some corporations give out tax-free monetary gifts for region-specific milestones, and military individuals receive deployment pay that is also tax-free. He says that by taking this tax-free money and investing it in a Roth IRA or a Roth TSP, you have not only obtained that money tax-free, but you can also grow it and withdraw it on a tax-free basis. You can also take that money and invest it in a SDP, which is a Savings Deposit Program, and earn a guaranteed 10% interest on up to $10,000.

For those who do not want to do the math, that is a free $1,000 every year on that principal deposit of $10,000.

Wayne Dyer, author of *Your Erroneous Zones*, says the first lesson he ever learned was to first pay yourself. He states that if you want to be financially independent by the time you hit your own midlife crisis, you have to make sure you are paying yourself first. This means that every investment you make has to be for yourself in your future, and he says that putting something away in savings is essentially paying yourself for the work you do now. He states that paying bills, eating food, and going out to movies are just rewards for living currently. If you want to pay yourself for the work you have done, then you have to set something aside in savings and investments in order to reap those benefits for the future.

Neil Godfrey, the author of *Money Doesn't Grow On Trees: A Parent's Guide To Raising Financially Responsible Children*, says you should step away from all the magazines and all the television that tell you things you think you need to know about the stock market. The only thing they do is show an individual how inept they are about the stock market because what these avenues are reporting on is something that has already happened. It is old news. If it has happened and existed for so long as to hit the media and hit print, then it is no longer viable advice for those investing in the stock market.

George Kender, who is a certified financial planner and founder of The Kinder Institute, says that it is not always about the money. For him, it has also been about the meaning. He has stated that many of the investments he has made over the course of his career have deep ties to what he thinks is most important in his life. Everything from estate planning to retirement planning to asset allocation has always been dependent upon what he feels holds the highest priorities within his life. However, do not confuse this point with being emotionally fueled, because they are two very different things. For example, if your stomach begins to growl, it means what should be important to you right now is food. However, is hunger an emotion? You might start to get frustrated because you are hungry at an inopportune time during the day, but hunger, in it of itself, is not an emotion. It is simply a need that needs to be fulfilled.

The hunger is important.

That is the difference between basing investments off of what is important versus basing investments off of emotionally fueled choices and decisions.

Alan Anderson

Rieva Lesonsky, co-author of *Start Your Own Business* and Senior Vice President and editorial director at *Entrepreneur* magazine, tells us that becoming debt-free is one of the best things you can do for your financial future. She stresses that investing in your savings, as well as your portfolio, while you are in debt is important, but relieving yourself of that debt as soon as possible enables you to stop throwing away money on interest and gives you more money you can then put towards your future investments.

After all, you have already learned how to live without that money in your pocket, but now that you are debt-free, you can utilize that money to work in your favor and work for your future.

Peter Navarro, prominent author and associate professor of economics and public policy at the University of California in Irvine, tells us to take every piece of advice we get from any financial investor, and toss it to the side. Many of those investors are trying to sell you specific things you probably do not want or need in order to have you as a client, and he states that if you want the best for your investments, you have to think of yourself despite what anyone else might tell you. For many people, investing in a particular financial advisor who promises things he or she cannot obtain results in lost money, unheard and unsolicited advice, and an unbalanced portfolio that does not work in the favor of the client.

Remember, even those who are in the advice-giving business are still in a business.

This is some wonderful advice from some of the most prominent experts in the field of stocks and investments. If this book and the information within it have overwhelmed you in any way, then rest assured that these are some wonderful tips you can fall back on from professionals who are not attempting to make money from you and simply want to help you succeed in the way they have seen success. Keep this chapter close to you whenever you find yourself lost in your own investment journey, and it will always provide a guiding light to get you out of whatever hole you feel you might have dug yourself into.

Above all else, remember this: you are the most important person when it comes to your investments.

Alan Anderson

Chapter 10: Dividend Investing

A portion of the earnings of a company is distributed among a class of shareholders. This portion is referred to as dividends. Dividend need not always be in cash; they could be in the form of stock or even property. Most stable companies pay dividends to their shareholders. Usually, the stock prices of financially secure companies tend to not move much, and they offer dividends to attract, reward, and hold on to the investors. If you are looking towards building long-term wealth, then investing in dividend-paying stocks is a good idea. In this chapter, you will learn about the basics of dividend investing.

Terms You Should Know

Cash Dividend

Cash dividends are cash payments that are made to the shareholders. These are paid on a "per share" basis, represented as a dollar amount or even as a percentage of the current market value of the share. Cash dividends are given out of the current earnings or the accumulated profits of any company.

Alan Anderson

Date of Record

The company makes use of this date for determining its shareholders (also referred to as holders of record).

Declaration Date

This is the date when the Board of Directors of a company would announce any upcoming dividend that is payable by the company.

Dividend

It is a portion of a company's earnings that it has decided to pay to its share or stockholders. Dividends can be paid out in the form of cash, stock, or even property. Dividends are payable only when a company earns profits. Only a particular class of shareholders is entitled to receive dividends.

Dividend Coverage Ratio

This is the ratio between the earnings of a company and the net dividends payable to the shareholders. This ratio helps the investors in measuring whether the earnings of a company are sufficient to cover its dividend obligations to the shareholders or not. Dividend coverage ratio is computed by dividing the earnings of each share by the dividend of each share.

Dividend Yield

This is a financial ratio that shows how much a company can pay out as dividends in a particular year. It's computed by splitting the annual payout for every share by the current price of the shares in the market.

Dividend Reinvestment Plan

This is also referred to as DRIP. This is a plan that is offered by a particular dividend-paying corporation that would enable the investor to automatically reinvest the cash dividends by subscribing to or by purchasing additional units of stock on the date of payment of dividend.

Ex-Dividend Date

The date on which or after which a stock is traded without any previous declaration of dividend

One Time Dividend

This is a special type of dividend that is declared in addition to the regular cash dividend that is paid.

Payment Date

This is the date when a declared dividend is scheduled for payment.

Shareholder

It could be an individual, company, or even an institution that owns at least one share in a particular company. A shareholder is also referred to as a stockholder.

Stock Dividend

These are dividends that are being paid in the form of additional shares or stock provided to the shareholders instead of being paid in cash.

Dividend Basics

A company that earns a profit can make use of that profit for three different purposes. It can reinvest that profit for expansion, that is, use it for the repurchase of its shares (debt reduction). It can make use of a portion of its profits to pay its shareholders. It can also reinvest it and payout to the shareholders as well. When the company wants to pay a portion of its profits to its shareholders, then it does so in the form of dividends. A dividend is a payment that's made to the shareholders, and depending upon the profits of the company, this payout can be made on a quarterly or yearly basis. Most businesses in the U.S. tend to pay dividends on a quarterly basis, whereas non-U.S. companies pay annual or bi-annual dividends.

Not all companies need to pay dividends to their shareholders. A company has the option of increasing, decreasing, or even eliminating the payment of dividends altogether, depending on its performance. For instance, if the company wants to free up its cash reserves to acquire another company, then it can reduce the payment of dividends. However, it is a general practice among companies to maintain or increase their dividend payouts to make sure that their shareholders stay happy and to avoid any form of negative publicity.

Dividends are declared on a per share basis. This means that the dividend that a shareholder would receive would depend on the number of shares that the he or she is holding. For instance, if you own 100 shares in a company and the company has declared an annual dividend of $4 per share, then the dividend that you would receive would be $400 ($4*100 shares). Not only this, but dividends are quoted according to the percentage of the actual market price of the stock. For instance, if a company announces a 4.5% dividend then the dividend payable would be equivalent to 4.5% of the current market price of the stock. The dividend payable to each eligible shareholder would be that percentage multiplied by the number of shares that are held by that shareholder at present. For instance, the stock of a company is being traded at $50 per share, and the company has declared a dividend of 5%. Then the dividend payable per share would be $2.50 per share ($50*2.5%).

The dividend yield for the stock is calculated by dividing the expected yearly dividend by the existing price of the stock: Dividend Yield = Annual Dividends per share/ price per share.

For instance, let us assume that the stock of ABC is being traded at $50 per share, and the company has offered an annual dividend of $5 per share. Then the dividend yield would be 10% ($5 dividend/ $50 per share). You will notice that if the stock were being traded at a higher price, then the dividend yield would decrease. If the stock is being traded at $100 per share, the dividend offered is $5, and then the dividend yield would be 5%. On the contrary, if the stock were being traded at a lower price, let's say $25, then the dividend yield would increase ($5 dividend/ $25 per share = 20% dividend yield). Please note that these instances are for illustrative purposes only.

It is quite easy to get enamored by companies that are offering high dividends. However, you will need to keep in mind that these figures, regardless of how impressive they are, are most often than not the indicators of very low future growth prospects. A very high dividend usually means that the company is facing some financial difficulty and that this would be accompanied by likely cuts in the future dividends. The stocks that have a low dividend yield often indicate an expectation of a high growth rate in the future. The historical average of the dividend yield of S&P 500 stocks has always been around 2% to 5%.

Cash Dividends, Stock Dividends, and One-Time Dividends

When someone talks about dividends, it usually refers to cash dividends. These are the cash payments that are made to the shareholders and are paid on the basis of the shares owned by them. This can be quoted in cash figures, like $5 per share, or even as a percentage of the current stock value, like 2.5%. The cash dividends are usually paid out of the current year's profits that a company earns or even from accumulated profits. Usually, the investors can reinvest these dividends for purchasing additional shares of the company's stock.

The stock dividends are given in the form of additional shares instead of cash. The number of additional shares that a shareholder would be entitled to would depend on the number of shares that the shareholder holds at present. For instance, a company could issue a stock dividend that is equal to five shares for every 100 shares that are held by a shareholder. If you were holding 500 shares currently, then you would be entitled to receive 25 additional shares. The stock dividend will lead to an increase in the number of shares being held by the shareholder, but this might not really have an immediate effect on the overall value of the shares held by such a shareholder.

A company has also got the option of paying a special dividend that is referred to as a one-time dividend. A company could declare this dividend for a variety of reasons. These reasons could range from a sudden increase in the cash holdings of a company resulting from the sale of a business or from any litigation earnings.

Dividend Dates

The Board of Directors of a corporation will have to declare all their dividends. There are four dates related to this declaration. Declaration date would be the date on which the dividend is being declared by the Board of Directors. This declaratory statement should include details about the size of the dividend, the date of the record, and the payment date. Once the company declares its dividend, then the company incurs a legal responsibility of paying it. The date of record or the record date is the date on which the same needs to be recorded in the company's books. On this date, the company will get to determine the holders of records (shareholders) and makes use of this date to determine to whom the financial reports, the proxy statements, and other required information need to be sent.

The ex-dividend date is also referred to as ex-date. Once the company has set its date of record, then the ex-dividend date will be set by either the stock exchange of the NASD (National Association of Securities Dealers). If an investor would purchase the stock on or after the ex-dividend date, then such a shareholder won't be qualified to receive the cash dividend that has been declared. However, those shareholders who have purchased the stock before the ex-date will be entitled to receive the dividend.

For better understanding, let us assume that a company has announced a cash dividend, and the ex-dividend date is December 7. If you have purchased 100 shares of this company on the 7th of December, then you will not be entitled to receive any dividend (on or after the ex-date). If you have purchased the shares on 5th December, then you will be entitled to receive the dividend that has been declared. The ex-dividend date is usually set for two days before the date of record.

A stock's price could increase as the ex-dividend date approaches. On the ex-date, the exchange can even reduce the price per share by the dollar amount of the dividend so declared. The payment date or the payable date is the date on which the declared dividend will need to be paid to the shareholders by the company. Only those shareholders who are holding the stock before the date of ex-dividend are the ones who will be entitled to receive this dividend.

Investing in Dividend Stocks

Most people tend to invest in dividend-paying stock to take advantage of the steady payments it promises and also for the reinvestment opportunity it offers for purchasing any additional shares. Most dividend-paying stocks represent the companies that are usually considered to be financially stable, and there is a scope for a steady increase in the dividends over a period of time. In the meantime, the shareholder gets to enjoy periodic payments in the form of dividends. For instance, a company might over a dividend of 2.5% in one year and increase it to 3% next year. However, this cannot be said with certainty. Once the company has earned the reputation of delivering reliable dividends that keep increasing with time, it will start working hard so as not to disappoint its investors.

A company that can consistently pay rising dividends is financially healthy and generates sufficient cash flow (as dividends are declared out of the cash earnings). Such companies are considered to be stable, and their stock prices aren't as volatile as that of other companies. Dividend-paying stocks are considered to be lower risk and are therefore more appealing to the younger investors who are looking forward to generating income in the long run, as well as the investors who are approaching retirement or are in retirement. It is a good source of income. The relationship between the share price and the dividend yield also helps in bolstering the investor's confidence. If there were a drop in the share prices, then the yield per share would increase.

Compounding

Dividends tend to provide the investors with the benefit of taking advantage of the power of compounding. Compounding takes place when earnings are generated, and the same is reinvested. This means earnings would be generated from further earnings. Dividend compounding takes place when dividends are reinvested for purchasing additional shares, thereby resulting in higher dividends.

For instance, let us assume that someone has asked you if you would rather take $1,000,000 right now or be given a penny that will double in value each day for a period of 30 days. Initially, the $1,000,000 would seem like a really good idea. However, after a little bit of number crunching, you might find that taking that penny would be better. So, you start out with $0.1 on the first day, it would become $0.02 on the second day, $.016 on the fifth day, $5.12 on the tenth day, $163.84 on the fifteenth day, $5242.88 on the twentieth day, $167,772 on the twenty-fifth day, and ultimately become $5,368,709.12 on the thirtieth day.

(Note: These figures are for purely illustrative purposes and show an exaggerated power of compounding.)

As you would have understood from the figures, the first couple of weeks aren't very eventful, and it would seem quite impossible that a penny could grow that significantly. Eventually, your earnings will start to increase, and the $1,000,000 will seem paltry by the end of the 30-day period. Well, this is just an illustration, and it isn't realistic. However, your investment will definitely double during the first couple of weeks, and it would be highly unrealistic to assume that you will be able to earn thousands of dollars every single day. This example simply shows that over a period of time, your money has the potential to grow, especially if you keep reinvesting it. This is referred to as the power of compounding.

When it comes to dividend investing, the more often you receive and reinvest the dividends you get, the higher your rate of return would be, not immediately but eventually. Let us take a realistic assumption. You have, for instance, purchased 100 shares of a company at the rate of $50 per share. Your total investment would be $5,000. In the first year, the company pays a dividend of 2.5%, and your earnings from dividend income would be $125. If the dividend keeps increasing by 5% every year (5% of the previous year's dividend), your investment would be valued at $11,226 dollars after a period of 20 years, assuming that there is no change in the price of the stock, and you have reinvested all the dividends you have received. Now, let us consider a situation where the company would pay a quarterly dividend instead of a yearly dividend. Your final value of the investment after a period of 20 years will be more than $11,650. This is a total gain of 133%. If you bump up your initial investment to $50,000, you will end up with $116,502 over a period of 20 years due to the power of compounding.

To make the most of the power of compounding, you will need an initial investment, the earnings from it, the reinvestment of these earnings, and time.

DRIPs

A plan for dividend reinvestment is usually referred to as DRIP. In this plan, the company will allow its investor to automatically reinvest all the cash dividends by purchasing any additional units of stock. This is a great way for investors to make full use of the compounding potential of the stock. Instead of receiving your check for quarterly dividends, the company or the entity managing the DRIP for the company would put this money, on your behalf, directly for the purchase of additional stock. Most DRIPs will allow you to purchase the additional shares sans any commission and maybe at a discounted price. DRIPs that are operated by the company don't levy a commission, as there is no broker involved in this process. There are certain DRIPs that would offer the shareholders the option to purchase these extra shares in cash, from the company directly, at a discount that could range from 1% to 10%.

The shares acquired in this manner are significantly cheaper because of the discount offered and the lack of a commission. From the company's point of view, DRIPs are quite attractive because these shares are directly sold by the company via a stock exchange. DRIPs also provide the company with the opportunity to raise further capital over a period of time while reducing the outflow of cash. All those investors who are in it for the long haul find this option quite attractive. From the perspective of an investor, DRIPs tend to offer a very convenient mode for reinvestment. The one drawback would be the taxes that the investor would need to pay the dividends reinvested, even though the shareholder never receives any cash per se.

Doing your Homework and Taxation

Like any other investment, it is necessary that you do your due diligence before taking any decision related to dividends. There are different factors that should consider while doing your research about selecting a dividend stock. This includes the dividend yield, dividend coverage ratio, and the company's history in terms of the payment of dividends.

Dividend Yield

As mentioned earlier, the dividend yield denotes the amount that the company can pay in dividends in relation to the price of shares. The higher the dividend yield, the better an investment it would be. However, this ratio can be quite deceptive. Keep in mind that this ratio tends to increase as the price of the share drops. If the dividend yield is high, this might be an indicator of a fall in the market price of the stock or that the future dividends might be cut off altogether. This would mean trouble for the investors. Not only will they lose money on the falling price of the stock, but they would also lose out on any future earnings in the form of dividends. Usually, investors tend to focus on the stocks with a dividend yield of 2% to 5% over a period of six decades.

Dividend Coverage Ratio

This is the ratio of the company's earnings and the net dividends declared to its shareholders. This ratio helps out the investors in measuring whether the earnings of a company would be sufficient for covering its dividend obligations. The dividend coverage ratio is calculated by dividing the earnings per share by the dividend per share: Dividend Coverage Ratio = Earnings per share/ Dividend per share.

For instance, a company with $10 earnings per share and that pays a dividend of 2.5% would have a dividend coverage ratio of 4. A company that has a coverage ratio that falls between 2 and 3 shows that it has adequate funds to meet its dividend obligation. If this ratio were less than 2, then it would mean that there might be a reduction in the dividends in the future. If this ratio were less than 1, this would indicate that the company is making use of its retained earnings or profits to pay for the current year's dividend. If the same ratio is more than 1, it means that the company is holding out on its investors and that it is capable of handing out greater dividends.

Continuous Record

Companies that have been giving out consistent dividends and dividends that show an upward curve are stable financially and are being managed well. However, a good track record doesn't guarantee an equally good performance in the future. This would definitely be a better investment than a company with an inconsistent dividend history. That being said, any company that pays a dividend must have paid its first dividend at some point in time or another. At times, companies take a while before making such payments. For instance, Microsoft didn't start paying out dividends until February 2003. That is about 17 years since it had made its IPO (Initial Public Offering) in the year 1986.

Online Research

Investors today have access to different online tools and screeners for evaluating various dividend stocks. A small fee would be charged for providing this information. However, most of the research can be performed at hardly any cost apart from the time that it would take for this research. There are certain websites that offer various screeners that will enable you to screen through different dividend stocks available based on various filters, such as the market cap, price, dividend payout, the frequency of dividends paid, industry or a specific sector, and also the company's performance history. Based on the various inputs, the screener will screen through all the dividend stocks and provide you information about stocks that would match your requirements. While investing, don't forget that investing in stock is never risk-free.

Taxes

Whenever a company is paying a dividend of $10 or above, it should provide you with an IRS Form 1099-DIV, Dividends and Distributions. The ordinary dividends are paid out of the earnings of a company and its profits. These are taxable as conventional dividends, unless they happen to be qualified dividends. Ordinary dividends to which rates of capital gains tax would be applicable to are referred to as qualified dividends. A qualified dividend would be one that is paid by a domestic U.S. company or a qualifying foreign company (that is incorporated in the possession of the U.S. or is eligible for any of the benefits provided under the comprehensive income tax treaty with the U.S.), as well as a company that is not listed with the IRS as a qualified dividend or hasn't met the required period of dividend holding.

You are required to report any earnings from dividends on your tax return. Line 9a or the Form 1040 or 1040A is where you will need to mention ordinary dividends, and qualified dividends are reported in line 9b. You will have to fill out Schedule B if you have received more than $1500 from ordinary dividends. According to your situation, you might have to fill out additional forms or schedules. You will need to pay projected taxes to avoid any interest or penalties if your dividends are significant. The federal income tax system is a pay-as-you-go tax system. This means that you will need to keep paying tax as and when you receive any income. An employer would usually hold back a certain sum from your monthly paycheck and send it to the IRS. If you haven't paid enough tax through these withholdings or if you have got other sources of income that aren't covered in these withholdings, you will need to pay the projected tax.

Dividend income can be considered as a source of income for which you will need to pay the projected tax. Usually, if you expect that you owe more than $1000 as tax, then you should consider making quarterly payments for estimated tax. Individuals can usually file Form 1040-Es, Estimated Tax for Individuals, along with the other appropriate estimated tax forms depending upon the state in which you live. The other option would be to submit a Form W-4 to the employer to change your withholding allowance. Tax laws keep changing; so make sure that you are up to date about the laws that are applicable to you. Alternatively, you can always get a professional to help you out with your taxes.

Most investors tend to take up dividend paying stocks for generating additional income and for the growth of their wealth. Like with any other investment, it is important that you have done your homework and have finalized those investments that would meet your objectives.

Positives and Negatives of Dividend Investing

The companies that pay dividends to its shareholders distribute a portion of their net income for this purpose and then reinvest the rest into their business operations. Given that these stocks provide regular income to their shareholders, this is an ideal way of investing an element of passive income into the investment portfolio. However, dividend stocks have certain pros and cons. Let's take a look into this.

Benefits of Dividend Investing

<u>Generating passive income</u>

Most investors are attracted to dividend stock because this provides them with a steady stream of income with little or no work. This is similar to the income from interest provided by a bank on an investment, but with a better potential for ROI (return on investment). However, you shouldn't keep expecting a dividend-paying company to make good on all their dividend payouts. This might sound slightly risky. It is a fact that a mature and a well-established company will keep paying dividends; however, there might not be a regular increase in these payouts. Stable dividends comprise a very important factor that will help ensure that the price of the stock stays strong, and if dividend-paying companies make it their priority to keep doing so, it would ensure their financial position.

Alan Anderson

Making the most out of compounding

Compounding is a really good way of increasing your earnings by generating further earnings. Through the process of compounding, you have the ability to earn extra income without investing any extra money from your pocket, thus making your earnings work for you. When it comes to making use of dividends for purchasing additional shares in a company, you will earn more money because every share that you acquire will receive its own dividend payout. This strategy is quite simple. Your original investment will generate a certain investment that can, later on, be invested again to increase your returns. The longer you do this, the higher your returns would be.

Invest once and profit twice

When you start investing in dividend stocks, you will profit in more ways than one. You are already aware of the regular payouts that you will be receiving; in addition to this, you should take into consideration the ROI you will receive when the price of the shares increases. Stocks that don't pay a dividend offer a potential for profit if you buy the shares at a low price and then sell them at a higher price. When it comes to dividend stocks, you get to share on the profits earned by the company while also holding on to the ownership of your investment. Given that most large companies handing out a dividend are financially reliable and stable, their stock prices are bound to increase over a period of time (provided the market conditions stay favorable).

Maximizing returns with dividend reinvestment

Reinvesting the earnings from dividends is quite an effective way of taking advantage of compounding. It can further be simplified if you start making use of DRIPs. As mentioned earlier, this will enable investors to automatically invest their cash dividends into more shares of the company. DRIPs help you make the most of compounding, as well as dollar-cost averaging. The automatic purchase of shares occurs on the dividend paying date of the company and can be managed either by the company itself or by an agent on its behalf. This allows you to purchase shares without any commission or even at a discounted price.

Drawbacks of Dividend Investing

Twice the taxation

One of the main drawbacks would be the amount of tax to which you would be subjected. You will be subjected to taxation even before you have received your dividend because the company will be issuing these from their net earnings, and it has to pay taxes on its annual earnings. You will be subject to taxation as an individual when you earn a dividend. This would be a personal income, and it is subject to taxation. Essentially, you are getting taxed twice – as an individual investor and also as a partial owner of the company.

Changes in dividend policy

The dividend policy would be the company's plan for determining the amount of dividend payable and any future increments based on its capacity for future earnings. When a company makes any changes to this policy, especially if it is regarding any cuts or an elimination of these payouts, then it would have a negative impact on the stock price of the company. There is a stock market theory that is known as the clientele effect, and it states that the stock price of a company is linked to the reactions of the investors when the company changes its policies. According to the changes in these policies, the investors would decide whether to buy or sell their shares. If due to any reason, a company is forced to slash down its dividends, then you are not only faced with the risk of losing your regular income from dividends, but the value of the shares that you are holding on to would also depreciate because the other shareholders are selling their stocks.

High dividend payout risk

Investing in businesses that have a high dividend payment percentage has a certain degree of risk. This ratio displays the company's ability to pay dividends out of its earnings. Determining the amount that needs to be paid to the shareholders is an art in itself. Given that most companies will not only want to attract new investors but also hold on to their existing ones, they give out higher payouts while at the same time trying to retain some of their earnings for future growth, further expansion, and also for raising the number of dividends payable. When this ratio is too high, then it becomes challenging for the company, and it might need to hold back or eliminate the payment of dividends.

Chapter 11: Advanced Investments

According to the existing Financial Conduct Authority rules, there are some investments that are considered to be complex. You will need to understand that the manner in which you deal with these differs substantially from dealing in other non-complex investments like shares and funds. If you haven't dealt with a particular complex investment in the past, then you will need to carry out an appropriateness assessment. There are different instruments, and they involve varying degrees of risk.

Warrants

A warrant is a time-bound right to subscribe for shares, debentures, government securities, or other loan stock. It is a right that is exercisable against the issuer of the underlying securities you are dealing in. Even if there is a relatively small movement in the price of an underlying security, it could lead to a large movement in the price of the warrant. This movement can either be favorable or unfavorable. The price of warrants is therefore considered to be volatile. If you are considering purchasing any warrants, then it is essential that you understand that the right to subscribe to warrants is time barred. This means that if the investor fails to exercise his or her right within the prescribed time frame, then the investment would become absolutely worthless.

Subscription Shares

These are quite similar to warrants. They also offer the shareholders the right to purchase shares at a later on a date or during the period of predetermined conversion at a specified price. However, unlike warrants, these qualify for the components of stocks and shares components of ISA and SIPPs (self-invested personal pensions). As a holder of these investments, an investor can decide whether he or she would want to subscribe for additional shares on the set dates. These signify a geared investment, so even a small change in the market price of the shares would result in a large positive or negative change in the market price of the subscription shares. Furthermore, the price of these instruments might not move in sync with the price of the underlying shares. This is due to the operation of the forces of demand and supply during the period of their existence. You stand the risk of losing out on your entire investment, as it could be worthless if the net asset value is less than the final excise price.

Securitized Derivatives

This instrument gives you a right to buy or sell investments that can be exercised against a person other than the actual issuer. However, this right is time barred. This could also provide you with rights under a contract for differences, thereby allowing for speculations on any fluctuations in the value of the property or an index, like the FTSE 100 index. In both of these cases, the investment or the property is referred to as an underlying instrument. These instruments usually have a higher degree of leverage. Thus, even a small change in the market rate of the shares would result in a large positive or a negative change in the market price of these instruments.

These instruments are quite volatile. They have a limited life (unless there is a guarantee for a return on the investment that you have invested in) and would be rendered useless if the underlying asset doesn't perform as anticipated.

Convertible Bonds

A convertible bond is a bond that has an option of being converted into equity. This would allow the investor to convert the bond into a given number of shares in the underlying company at a predetermined price. Throughout the specified lifetime of the bond, the holder would keep receiving a regular dividend. However, this would be at a lower rate than that which is associated with a majority of bonds. At any given point of time within the lifetime of the bond, the holder has the right to convert these bonds into the proportionate number of underlying shares. The conversion takes place at the convenience of the holder, and it cannot be forced upon the holder by the issuing company. Given that these bonds have got the option of conversion, they are viewed as having a rooted call.

Convertible Preference Shares

This particular form of investment is quite similar to convertible bonds. The investor has the option of converting these preference shares into the underlying ordinary shares. As they come with the option of conversion, they are regarded as being embedded with a call option. The risk that the investor should be aware of is the volatility of the regular market conditions. Akin to the holder of convertible bonds, even a holder of preference shares is ranked above an ordinary shareholder when it comes to repayment. However, other bondholders outrank them.

Exchange Traded Commodities

These are also referred to as ETCs for the sake of convenience. These enable the investor to keep a track of the performance of the commodity index, including the total return index or indices. The trading of these instruments is similar to that of regular shares. As the prices are available through the entire trading day, with the support of the market maker, this stimulates their liquidity. ETCs either focus on a single commodity or on a particular index. Examples would be gold or silver for an individual commodity exposure or energy and livestock for exposure to an index. ETCs would permit an investor to invest in a class of assets that have previously been regarded as being off-limits for a regular investor.

Historically speaking, commodities have been an integral part of institutional investment strategies. However, three conditions lead to these commodities being out of the reach of an investor. These conditions are contingent liability, margining requirements, and international exchanges. There can be sudden oscillations in the price of these investments because of the nature of the underlying commodities in which the investments are made. This class of investments isn't for the faint-hearted. These fluctuations would have an immediate and a direct impact on the prices of the shares they represent.

Nil Paid Rights

At times, companies might decide that they would want to raise more funds from their shareholders for an additional issue of shares. This is referred to as rights issue. If an existing shareholder wants to decline this right that is allocated to him or her, then he or she has the option of selling the rights to these new shares "nil paid" (that is, without paying any further amount to the company), or he or she can let the right lapse (in this case, the company would itself sell these rights on behalf of the investor and will remit any amount from such proceeds to the concerned investor). This would provide all the purchases in the open market with an opportunity to buy shares at a discounted price during the rights issue. This means that the new investor has acquired a timed "call" option (lasts for a maximum of 21 days), and this can be exercised within the stipulated time.

Structured Products

The needs of an investor that cannot be met by the regular financial instruments that are available in the market are met by structured products. These have been used as an alternate option for direct investments and also as part of the process of asset allocation to reduce the risk and exposure that exists within the portfolio. The basic concept is to have an investment that exists within a derivative with an additional feature of protection if it is held until maturity. There are risks involved in it, and you shouldn't treat them lightly. These risks arise due to different combinations of derivatives and other financial instruments.

Warrants

A warrant is similar to an option. The holder has the right – but not an obligation – to buy the underlying security at a specified price and quantity at some time in the future. An option is an instrument that is traded on the stock exchange, whereas a warrant will be issued by a company. The security that is represented by the warrant (it usually happens to be an equity share) will be delivered by the company issuing it instead of the investor holding those shares. Warrants are usually included by companies as a part of their new issue offering. This is offered to attract investors and to improve the confidence of a shareholder in the stock. This is conditional to any actual increase in the value of the underlying security over a period of time. A warrant is a kind of equity derivative. There are different types of warrants, namely, call warrants and put warrants. A call warrant denotes a specified number of shares that an investor can purchase from the issuer at a given price, on or before a pre-decided date. On the other hand, a put warrant denotes a specific number of equities that can be sold to the issuer at a pre-decided price, on or before the expiration of a certain period.

Characteristics of a Warrant

The particulars of a warrant certificate would depend on the different invest tools that they are representing. All warrants have an expiration date; this is the last day on or before which the rights of a warrant can be exercised. Depending on the manner in which they can be exercised, they can be classified as well. For instance, an American warrant can be exercised at any time before its expiration period, whereas a European warrant can be exercised only on the date of expiration. The instrument that the warrant represents will be stated on the warrant certificate. A warrant represents the corresponding number of underlying shares. However, it can also represent a commodity, any currency, or even an index.

The exercise price is also referred to as the strike price, and it is the amount that will need to be paid for buying or selling the call and put warrant, respectively. When the strike price has been paid, it results in the transfer of the specific number of underlying securities it represents. The conversion ratio helps in determining the number of warrants that would be required for buying or selling one unit of the investment. For instance, if the conversion ratio for buying stock of a company was 3:1, this would imply that the investor will need to have three warrants to purchase one share. If the conversion ratio happens to be high, it usually implies a low share price and vice versa. An index multiplier would be stated on the certificate in case of an index warrant. This figure will help in determining the amount that would be payable to the holder on the exercise date.

Warrants are transferable instruments; they can vary from medium to long term and have quoted certificates. These are high-risk and offer high return as well. Warrants present a really good option for all the speculators and hedgers in the market. These are quite viable for private investors and are transparent in their nature of operations. The cost of warrants is usually low, and the initial investment that is required is comparatively small as well.

Advantages of a Warrant

Let us take into consideration an example in order to gain a better understanding of the benefits offered by a warrant. For instance, the shares of a company have a market value of $1.50 per share. You will need to invest $1500 to purchase 1000 shares. However, if the investor opted to invest in warrants (where one warrant represents one share) that were priced at $.50 per warrant, such an investor would be in ultimate possession of 3000 shares for the same investment.

The leverage and the gearing that are offered by warrants tend to be high due to their low price. This would mean that the potential for reaping capital gains would be larger. It is quite common that the warrant and share price might be moving in a parallel manner. However, the proportion of likely gain or loss will differ significantly due to the initial difference in their pricing.

Another illustration will help in gaining a better understanding of this concept. For instance, the share of a company records a gain of $.30 per share from the initial price of $1.50; thus, it would be $1.80. This shows a 20% gain. However, if the price of a warrant goes from $.30 to $.80, this would indicate a 60% hike. In the given situation, the gearing factor is arrived at by dividing the initial price of the share by the initial price of the warrant ($1.50/$.50 = 3). The gearing factor is 3, and this shows the financial leverage offered by the warrant. The greater this number is, the higher potential for capital gains (or losses).

During a bullish market, the gains offered by warrants are quite significant. They also provide the investor with protection during a bearish market. As the price of the underlying shares drops, the warrants probably wouldn't realize the same loss as compared to the underlying shares. This financial leverage comes in quite handy.

Disadvantages

Warrants have certain drawbacks and risks, just like any other investment. The leverage that's offered by this instrument is often high. However, this could work to the investor's disadvantage as well. Let us take into consideration the example that was mentioned above. If you have realized a drop of $.30, then the percentage of loss of the share would be 20%, and that incurred on a warrant would be 60%. An increase is always favorable; however, a drop in the same price could prove to be a greater disadvantage. The next risk that the investor would face would be that the value of a warrant certificate could plummet to zero as well. If this happens before the rights were to be exercised, then the warrant wouldn't have any redemption value. A warrant doesn't carry any voting rights. The investor won't have a say in any matters regarding the functioning of the company, although his or her rights would be affected by the company's decision.

Subscription Shares

Subscription shares can be considered to be a variation of warrants. They help in providing the investor with a geared exposure towards the growth of capital of a company. They are a distinct class of shares and have distinct rights specific to them. Subscription shares share a few characteristics with warrants. Just like warrants, subscription shares have the right (although it isn't an obligation) for conversion into regular shares on a specific date in the future or during a specific period at a price that's been fixed beforehand. These shares are considered as regular share capital for purposes of taxation. To provide these shares with some liquidity, they should be listed with the listing authority. An investor would obviously want to convert his or her subscription shares to ordinary shares in the issuer's company if the trading prices are more than the exercise price. Therefore, it is safe to say that the success of the issue of subscription shares for raising new capital would depend on the performance of the share prices.

Subscription shares provide the shareholders with a form of tradable securities that can be converted into ordinary shares that would assist in the future growth of the company; the same could be realized for cash as well. Working on the assumption that the subscription shares would be converted into regular shares, the capital base of the issuer will improve. This would allow the distribution of costs of operations over a greater number of ordinary shares, and the total expense ratio will decrease as well.

The subscriptions shares would be given the same treatment as warrants for the purposes of listing. The number of warrants and other options for subscribing to equity shares cannot go beyond 20% of the issued equity share capital of the issuer. Usually, subscription shares are issued based on a "one for five" basis so that the issuer will not have any warrants or options that are outstanding for subscribing to its ordinary share capital. Normally, these shares are issued by the way of a bonus issue to its existing investors holding ordinary shares at present. In addition to this, they can be issued as a part of placement for offering new shares with the attachment of subscription shares.

Subscription shares can qualify for stocks and shares constituent of an ISA, unlike warrants. This is perhaps the main reason for their popularity. The conversion price that is paid while exercising the right to convert subscription shares into ordinary shares will be used to calculate the annual subscription limit for the year in which this right of conversion has been exercised, unless this price was already paid out in the form of cash that is held within the stock and shares ISA of the shareholders. These shares can also be held by the investor in the form of SIPPs. Subscription shares are regarded as share capital, and their particular rights are included in the AOA of the company issuing it. Meanwhile, warrants aren't regarded as share capital, and their related rights would be contained in the warrant instrument itself.

The company can make use of the balance in the share premium account, the capital redemption reserve, and the profit and loss account for issuing subscription shares through a bonus issue. Usually, for the purposes of taxation, companies tend to use their share premium account. If the right of conversion of subscription shares isn't exercised within the given period, then the right of conversion will expire. If the subscription shares tend to expire while the regular shares are being traded at a premium to the price of conversion, then a trustee would be appointed by the issuer.

There are two reasons for this appointment. It would either be for exercising the right and for selling the resultant shares in the market or for accepting any other available offers for the purchase of any of the outstanding subscription shares. The proceeds from either of these transactions will be remitted to the shareholders of the subscription shares. If this period expires when the ordinary shares are being traded at a price that is less than the conversion price, then the trustee will not take any action, and the right of subscription will be considered to have lapsed.

As is the case with any other class of shares, even subscription shares can confer any type of rights. Subscription shareholders are usually given the right to receive dividends. Subscription shareholders have limited voting rights, and this would prevent the issuer from taking a particular action without obtaining the prior permission of the holders of such shares. However, they don't get to vote at any of the general meetings of the issuing company.

Convertible Bonds

New investors often wonder what convertible bonds are all about and if they are bonds or stocks. These are corporate bonds that can, later on, be converted into common stock by the holder of this instrument. As is obvious from the name, these convertible bonds offer the holder an option of converting the bonds into a fixed number of shares of the issuing company.

Initially, these convertible bonds perform like any other corporate bonds but with an interest rate that is slightly lower. However, these convertibles can then be converted into stocks that would benefit from an increase in the price of the underlying shares. If the shares perform poorly, then there wouldn't be any conversion, and the investor would have to make peace with a poor return.

Similar to any other investment, there is a tradeoff between risk and return in this instrument as well. The conversion ratio will help in calculating the number of shares that the holder is likely to receive when the bonds have been converted into the underlying stock. The indenture includes the conversion ratio, along with all the other necessary provisions. Usually, the price or the value of the bond would increase when the stock reaches the conversion price. At this given point, the convertible bonds would behave like the stock option. If the stock price starts to increase or becomes volatile, then your bond will behave in the similar fashion. A convertible bond will closely follow the movement of the underlying stock. The only exception would be when the share price falls down substantially. If that's the case, then at the time of maturity of the bond, the bondholders will receive an amount that's not below the par value of the instrument.

The company that is issuing these bonds has the right to call. This means that the company issuing them can convert them, forcibly if need be. Forced conversion occurs when the stock price is more than the amount it would be had the bond been redeemed, or it could also occur on the call date of the bond. This feature tends to place a cap on the potential of appreciation of the instrument.

As previously mentioned, convertible bonds are considered to be complex securities for a couple of reasons. They have the combined features of bonds and stocks. This might be confusing for investors initially. Investors have to take into consideration all the different reasons that would affect convertible bond prices. These factors include any changes in the interest rates and the market for the underlying securities. Moreover, they need to take into consideration the fact that these can be called up by the investor at a particular price, and this could insulate the issuer from any significant rise in the share price. These investments will seem more complex than they actually are if you start getting overwhelmed by all their intricacies. To put it simply, convertibles provide the investor with a security blanket of sorts that will help him or her in

Alan Anderson

participating in the growth of a concerned company.

There are different advantages and disadvantages that you should be aware of while making use of these securities. Convertible bonds are considered to be a deferred method of equity financing. The advantage of this would be a dilution of the common stock and also the earnings per share or EPS. Another advantage would be that the company would be able to offer the bond at a lesser value than what it would have had to pay on a regular bond. Regardless of the profitability of the company, the holders of these convertible bonds will receive a fixed income, that is, a limited income until they are converted. This is a benefit for the company because a bigger chunk of the operating income would be made available for the regular shareholders. The company will only have to share its operating income with the shareholders who have recently converted their instruments.

Holders of these bonds don't usually get to vote for directors. The option of voting is available to the common stockholders. Thus, if the company wasn't looking for an alternative financing means without diluting the control of its business, then issuing convertible bonds would be a good idea. However, this is a temporary advantage.

Moreover, the bond interest can be shown as a deductible interest for the company issuing it. Thus, convertible bonds have more advantages than equity and preferred shares for a corporation that is looking for ways to finance additional capital. For an issuer, these convertible bonds have a higher risk of bankruptcy than regular stock options. Furthermore, these instruments have a shorter maturity period, and the risk involved is greater. By making use of fixed income securities, the losses incurred would be magnified for all the stockholders when the sales and the earnings decrease. This would be the downside of the financial leverage they offer.

The restrictive provisions on these convertible bonds are strict when compared to those of other short-term credit options available. Making use of heavy debt will also affect the ability of a company to finance its operations during stressful economic situations. During these times, the investors might be reluctant to lend funds unless it is in the form of secured loans.

Convertible Preference Shares

When you are investing in stocks, there is always the risk of losing out on your investment. However, avoiding stocks altogether would mean that you would be missing out on a good opportunity to make some money. There is one type of security that will help solve this dilemma that every investor faces. Convertible preference shares provide the investor with the assurance of a fixed return while providing a chance for capital appreciation in the future. In this section, you will learn more about convertible preference shares.

Convertible preference shares are a form of fixed income securities issued by a corporation that will provide the investor with the option to turn these securities into a specific number of shares of the issuing company after the expiration of the time frame for which they have been issued or on a specific date. The component of fixed income would provide the investor with a steady income and also some form of protection for his or her investment. However, the option of converting these securities into the underlying shares will provide the investor with an opportunity to profit from the rise in the share price. These investments are appealing to all those investors who would want to participate in the growth of the company while being protected from any significant drop in the price of the stocks (if the stock doesn't perform like intended).

Let us take an example to understand how these convertible preference shares work and the manner in which the investors would benefit from them. Let us assume that a company has issued 1 million convertible preference shares at the rate of $100 per share. These convertible preference shares will provide the holder with a priority over the regular shareholders in two different ways. First, the convertible preference shareholders will be entitled to receive a dividend of 4.5% (if the earnings of the company prove to be sufficient) before any of the dividends are paid to the shareholders. Second, the holders of convertible preference shares would be prioritized over the common stockholders in the repayment of capital if the company goes bankrupt and its assets need to be liquidated.

That being said, the holders of convertible preference shares rarely have any voting rights, unlike common stockholders. By investing in these convertible preference shares, the worst that could happen to the investor would be that he or she would receive an annual dividend of $4.50 per share that they own. These securities will also provide their owner with the possibility of higher returns. If there is an increase in the value of the convertible preference shares of the company, then they can cash in on this by converting their investment into equity of the company. On the expiration date or the date of conversion, the shareholders would have the opportunity to convert either some or all of their convertible preference shares into common shares of the issuing company.

Determining the Profit on Their Conversion

The number of common shares that investors would receive for every convertible share that they hold is represented by the conversion ratio. Before the issue of the convertible shares, the management gets to determine the conversion ratio.

In continuation of the above illustration, let us assume that the conversion ratio is 6.5. This would allow the holder to trade these convertible shares for 6.5 of the common stocks of the issuing company. The conversion ratio would show the price at which the convertible securities can be traded for common stock for making a profit. This price is referred to as conversion price, and it is equal to the purchase price of the preferred share divided by the conversion ratio that is provided.

For instance, the conversion price in the abovementioned company would be $100/6.5 = $15.38. This means that the common stock of the company would need to be traded above $15.38 if the investor wants to make a profit on conversion. If the shares are converted, and the price of these shares falls down that price, then the investor would suffer a loss on his or her investment. If the value of the common stock closes at $10 per share, then the preferred shareholder will only receive $65 worth of common shares in return for his or her preferred shares valued at $100.

Securitization

Securitization is the process of creating a financial instrument by combining different financial assets and then marketing these different tiers of securities to investors. This process can comprise different types of financial assets, and it also helps in promoting liquidity in the market. Securities that are backed by mortgage would be a perfect instance of securitization. By clubbing up the mortgages, the issuer can then divide this huge pool into smaller parts based on the risk of default of each of these individual mortgages and then resell these smaller portions to the investors.

This process helps in creating liquidity by letting smaller investors acquire shares that form a part of the bigger asset pool. By making use of mortgaged-backed securities, the individual investor can purchase a part of the mortgage as a kind of bond. Without securitization, the individual investor might not be able to afford to buy into the bigger pool of mortgages present. The company that is holding the loans is referred to as the originator, and it would gather the necessary data on different assets that it would take out from related balance sheets. These assets would then be gathered together based on factors like the time period remaining on the loan, the risk involved, and so on. This group of assets that have been gathered together will then be sold to an issuer. The issuer will then create a set of tradable securities representing a stake in the associated assets and will, in turn, sell the same to investors who are interested at a particular rate.

Securitization will provide creditors with a means of lowering associated risks through the division of the ownership of the obligations of debt. The investors would get to assume the position of a lender by purchasing the security. The investor gets to earn a return that is based on the principle of association and the payments towards interests that are made by the debtors under their obligation. Unlike other forms of investments, this particular type of investment is based on tangible goods. In the case of a default in payment by the debtor, then the underlying asset can be seized and sold to compensate for the default in payment. Similar to any other investment, the higher the risk involved, the higher the potential returns would be.

Exchange Traded Commodity

Exchange traded commodities are referred to as ETCs, and they give the trader and the investor an exposure to commodities via shares. These are traded like a stock, that is, they are traded in a stock exchange.

ETCs track the movement of the price of the underlying commodity, such as oil, silver, and even gold, and their prices would fluctuate depending on the value of these underlying commodities.

ETCs can track individual commodities or even a basket of commodities. For instance, an ETC basket would be an instrument that would track multiple metals instead of one, or it can even track different agricultural commodities like wheat, soybeans, and corn.

The structure of ETCs can vary depending on the issuing company. There are certain exchanges around the world, like the London Stock Exchange and the Australian Securities Exchange, which would offer ETCs with a specific structure. These ETCs would track the price of the commodity. There would be a management fee that would be charged, and this would be the compensation for the company that's running these instruments.

ETCs would provide a net asset value, and this is the fair value of an ETC. ETCs are traded on a stock exchange and their market value can fluctuate above or below the NAV.

The commodity market could be a physical or a virtual marketplace for trading in commodities. There are about 50 commodity markets that are present around the world, and there are about 100 commodities that are traded on them. The commodities can be categorized as hard and soft commodities. Natural resources that can be mined or extracted, such as gold, rubber, and oil, would be examples of hard commodities. Soft commodities, on the other hand, would be agricultural products or even livestock like corn, wheat, pork and so on.

There are different ways in which you can invest in commodities. The stock can be purchased in corporations with a business that is dependent on commodity prices or even invest in mutual funds or ETFs that focus on companies related to commodities. A direct way of investing in these investments would be by buying a futures contract. A futures contract would place an obligation of buying or selling the commodity at a specific price on the date of delivery sometime in the future. The major commodity exchanges in the U.S. are concentrated in Chicago and New York.

Structured Products

Structured products have been designed to facilitate customized risk-return goals. This is made possible by taking any regular security, such as the conventional bond, and then replacing the usual features of payments with a couple of unconventional payoffs that are derived not from the cash flow of the issue, but from the performance of the underlying assets.

The return on these investments would depend on the performance of the underlying assets. If the return on the underlying asset is "x," then the payout on the structured product would be "y." This means that the performance of the structured product would be related to the traditional model of option pricing, even though they might contain other types of derivatives, such as swaps, forwards, and even futures, as well as several embedded features like downside buffers. Structured products have become popular in European markets, and they have gained popularity in the U.S. as well. In the U.S., they are made available as products registered with SEC; this means that they would be available to investors in the same manner as stocks, bonds, ETFs, and even mutual funds. It's the ability of these investments to offer customized exposure to usually hard-to-reach classes and subclasses of assets that would make these structured products a useful component of a diversified portfolio.

Let us look at an example to gain a better understanding of how these instruments function. For instance, a popular bank has issued these structured products in the form of notes, where each of these notes has a face value of $1000. Each note would be a package that would comprise two components, like a zero-coupon bond and a call option on the underlying instrument and like the common stock or an ETF that would mimic a popular index like the S&P 500 with a maturity period of three years.

The pricing of this instrument is complex; however, the principle involved is quite simple. On the date of issue, you will have to pay the face value, that is, $1000 per note. This would be a principal protected investment, which means you will get the $1000 you have invested on maturity, regardless of what would happen to the underlying asset.

Now, let us look at the performance aspect of this instrument. Let us assume that the underlying asset happens to be a European call option. The return you will earn would depend on the value of the investment at the date of its maturity. If this happens to be higher than the issuing value, then in such a case, you will earn a profit in addition to the original principal. However, if the option is worthless on the date of expiration, you will just receive your original principal without any additions to it. This means you will get your $1000 back on maturity.

In the abovementioned example, the key feature is the protection of the principal. In a different situation, the investor might be willing to trade all or some of this protection offered in favor of a performance feature that is more attractive. Consider another scenario. The investor wants to trade off the principal protection for a combination of other performance features.

A common risk that all structure products possess would be the lack of liquidity due to the customized nature of these investments. Until the date of the maturity, the full return from this investment cannot be realized. This is the reason why structured products tend to be an investment decision that goes along the lines of "buy and hold."

Apart from liquidity, the other risk associated with this form of investment would be the credit quality of the issuer. The cash flow is derived from other sources; the product on its own is considered to be a liability of the financial institution that is issuing it. Moreover, there is no transparency in the pricing strategies. That is, there is no uniform pricing standard for these investments. This would be difficult for making a comparison different structured offering.

These are all the different investment options that are available to an investor who is looking to invest in the not-so-traditional instruments. There are various advantages and disadvantages for each of these instruments. So, take into consideration all these before investing. Depending on your investment goals, you can accordingly decide which of these investments you would want to invest in. These complex securities will help in diversifying your portfolio. You will learn more about diversification of the portfolio and its benefits in the coming chapters.

Alan Anderson

Chapter 12: Passive Investing Vs. Active Investing

A passive investor is interested in investing for the long haul. A passive investor tends to limit the buying and selling going on within his or her portfolio, thereby making this quite cost effective. You will need to possess a buy and hold mentality for this. You will need to keep resisting the temptation of reacting or anticipating the next move of the stock market. An example of passive approach would be to acquire an index fund that would follow a major index, like the Dow Jones or the S&P 500. Whenever the constituents are switched up in these indices, the index funds that are following them also tend to switch up their holdings. Their holding would be switched up by selling the stock that is going out and acquiring such stock that is becoming a part of the index. This is the reason why it is a big deal when any company gets included in one of the major indexes in the world. This position would give it the guarantee that its stock will become a core investment in various major funds. When you have many small bits of stocks, you will earn returns on them by simply being a part of its upward trajectory. A successful passive investor will have to ignore any short-term setback, however big it is, and keep his or her eyes on the prize.

Like the name suggests, active investing is about taking a proactive approach towards building a portfolio. The main aim of actively managing money would be to take advantage of the fluctuations in the short-term prices of an investment. This needs a deeper understanding and analysis of the market so that you will know when to step into or out of a specific stock or investment. A portfolio manager will need to take a long and a hard look at various qualitative and quantitative factors to determine when and how the price would change. Active investing requires confidence about buying and selling at the right moment. If you want to be good at active investment, you will need to be more right than wrong.

So, which one would help in making the investor more money? If you look at the performance, then passive investing tends to be more helpful. There have been numerous studies, and none of them were in favor of active managers. In fact, only a small fraction of funds that are actively managed tend to perform better than the passively managed ones. Active and passive investing techniques happen to be two sides of the same coin. They both have their own pros and cons.

The hedge fund industry would be a really good example of this. Managers of hedge funds are renowned for their ability to sense the slightest change in the price of an asset. Typically, a hedge fund would avoid regular mainstream investments. However, the amount being invested by hedge funds in passive funds has been steadily growing over the last decade. Clearly, there are some reasons why passive and active investing are good.

Passive Investing

When compared to active funds that make use of managers for selecting the best investments out of the lot, passive investments simply try to replicate the performance of an index, usually by holding on to most or all of its constituents. There are pros and cons for each of these investing methods.

Finding an active fund manager with good judgment and experience is quite a difficult task. Let us take a look at the different pros and cons of passive investing.

Advantages of Passive Investing

The main benefit of passive investing would be the costs involved. The annual charges are quite nominal. If an investor is looking forward to minimizing the annual charges, then passive investing is a good strategy.

If you have any older tracker funds present in your portfolio, it is worth the checking charges. Some of the older passive funds tend to have a slightly high annual cost; sometimes, it is over 1%, which is not competitive these days. Investors in such funds should consider other alternatives because the high charge would just be an added burden on the performance, and in the long run, it could yield poor results.

The simplicity of passive investments is another advantage. Investors tend to feel comfortable with these funds because they know what they will be getting. They would be getting an investment that aims at aping the index. A major chunk of active fund managers tend to underperform. Thus, there is scope for underperformance while taking the active route. Over the long run, a passive approach will also underperform when compared to the benchmark set due to charges, regardless of how small they are. However, the diffusion of returns from various other actively managed funds would be much wider. In the long run, the passive investing technique seems to work better.

Disadvantages of Passive Investing

There are certain disadvantages of passive investing as well. One of the major risks of passive investing that usually goes unnoticed is concentration. Markets consist of a wide array of companies; they are usually concentrated towards the largest ones. In some cases, the indices tend to be overexposed towards one or several small stocks or sectors that have a large impact on their performance.

In most developed markets, the concentration of individual stock is not an issue. However, you would still find yourself being skewed towards a particular section or sector. In the 90s, when stocks of technology and telecoms started to become a large part of the FTSE 100, index and tracker funds certainly benefited from their growth, until it all went tumbling down. Then, the dominant component was financial, and then the mining shares got all the attention.

The dominant sector isn't always the best option that is available for you. You wouldn't want a major chunk of your portfolio invested in the so-called dominant sectors because the chances of them underperforming are quite high. The beta funds are aimed at helping mitigate this problem by helping weigh out these stocks or by making use of other factors, such as their value, momentum of price, or their volatility. However, there are no guarantees that these strategies would work.

There is another aspect that you should be mindful of when it comes to passive investment. Passive funds aren't sensitive towards valuation and other fundamental analysis of companies. The larger the sum of passive money, the greater the anomalies present in the market would be.

Active Investing

There are many advantages that active investing has to offer. Active investing helps provide flexibility. Active investors don't need to follow a specific index. They have the autonomy to buy such stocks or make such investments that they think have potential. Active managers also get to hedge their bets by making use of different techniques, such as short sales or even put options. When the risk starts getting bigger, they can also exit any specific stock or sector.

Passive managers are usually stuck with the stocks that are held in the index that they are tracking, regardless of their performance. This is also a good method of tax management. The losses incurred from selling one investment can be set off against a profitable one.

However, even an active investing strategy has certain shortcomings. This is quite expensive. The expenses incurred for maintaining an actively managed equity fund is on the higher side when compared to a passive equity fund. Given all the active buying and selling involved, the transaction costs also tend to be high, and this causes the fees to be high as well. Well, you will also be paying for the services offered to you by the analysts who have helped you pick out the investments. All these fees can add up to a huge sum that would make the point of investing seem worthless.

Active managers can buy any investment that they think would generate high returns. When the analysts are right, then it produces amazing results. However, when they get it wrong, things can go south pretty quickly.

The best investment strategy would be the perfect blend of active and passive styles of investing. You don't necessarily have to choose between either a passive or active style; instead, making a portfolio by combining these two techniques will help in diversification and mitigation of risk.

Chapter 13: Analysis

Fundamental Analysis

The method of evaluating a security to measure its intrinsic value by taking into consideration various related factors is referred to as fundamental analysis. The other things that need to be considered are various qualitative and quantitative factors and other economic and financial factors.

A fundamental analyst will need to perform a detailed study about anything that could affect the value of a security. This would include an analysis of various macroeconomic factors as well, such as the conditions in the economy and the industry. The microeconomic factors also need to be evaluated. The aim of a fundamental analysis would be to provide the investor with quantitative data that will help him or her understand whether the security has been over or under-valued.

Fundamental analysis helps in determining the well-being of a company by taking into account various key numbers and other economic indicators. The purpose of doing so is to identify companies that are fundamentally strong and distinguishing these from those companies or industries that are fundamentally weak. This method of analyzing securities is said to be the exact opposite of technical analysis.

All the real and public data that is available is utilized for analyzing and evaluating the value of a security. Most analysts tend to make use of this technique for the valuation of stocks. However, the same method could be used for the valuation of any security.

For instance, a fundamental analysis can be performed on a bond by considering various economic factors, such as the rates of interest and the overall economic conditions. Revenue earned, future growth prospects, the return on equity, profit margins, and other related data are used when analyzing stocks and other equity instruments. When it comes to stocks, fundamental analysis tends to focus on the financial statements of a company that need to be evaluated.

Technical Analysis

Technical analysis is about forecasting the price movements of an investment based on the analysis and examination of the past prices and its movements. Akin to weather forecasting, technical analysis doesn't produce results that are absolute. Technical analysis can help an investor in anticipating what is "likely" to happen to the price range. This makes use of a wide array of charts to show the price movements over a period of time. This analysis is applicable to different things, such as stocks, commodities, futures, and any other tradable instrument. Any such instrument that can be influenced by the forces of demand and supply that operate in the market can be analyzed by making use of this technique.

The Dow Theory helped lay down the foundations for the present-day technical analysis. The Dow Theory is the compilation of the writings of Charles Dow over a period of several years. The three theorems or ideas that form the basis of this theory are explained below.

Price can discount everything. A technical analyst would believe that the current price would reflect all the information that is required. The price would reflect the sum of the knowledge of all the different market participants.

The movements of price aren't random. There is a trend to these movements, and most technicians would agree to this. However, there are certain periods when there is no trend per se, and technicians would agree to this as well. If prices were as random as people think they are, then it would be difficult to make any money by making use of this analysis. A technician would always function under the belief that he or she will be able to identify a trend in the market. Investment decisions can be then made based on such trends.

Technical analysis can be applied to both short- and long-term investing. "What" is definitely more important than "why." Technical analysts are usually concerned with only two things, and these are the current price and the history of the movement of the price.

The current price of an investment is attributed to the constant battle that takes place between the forces of supply and demand that operate in the market. The aim of this analysis is to identify the direction in which the price of an investment would head in the future. This analysis is more of a direct approach than technical analysis. Fundamental analysts are usually concerned with trying to figure out the reasons as to why the price is what it is.

The general steps that are usually followed by a technical evaluation are as follows: The first step would be to conduct a broad market analysis by making use of different major indices, like NASDAQ, Dow Industrials, or even the NYSE. The next step would be to perform a sector analysis. A sector analysis will help in identifying the strongest and the weakest groups that exist within the market. The final step would be the performance of individual stock analysis for identifying the strongest and the weakest stocks present in the selected groups.

This analysis is quite versatile, and its principles are universally applicable. Performing a technical analysis takes skill and practice. It would be advisable that you hire some professional help for this.

Chapter 14: Portfolio Diversification

Benefits of Diversification

A technique that helps in reducing risk by distributing it among different financial instruments is referred to as diversification. This helps in maximizing returns by investing in different areas that would, in turn, react in different ways to the same event. Diversification helps in reducing the risk of a loss, but it doesn't prevent a loss.

There are two main types of risks that you will need to watch out for while investing. The first one is known as undiversifiable risk. This is also referred to as systematic risk, and it is associated with every company. The various causes of this are inflation, rates of exchange, political stability, and rates of interest. This isn't peculiar to one type of company or industry, and it cannot be eliminated or even reduced through diversification. Investors will need to simply accept it and put up with it.

The second risk is referred to as diversifiable risk. This is also referred to as unsystematic risk, and it is certainly specific to a particular company, market, or an economy. Business and financial risks are the most common sources of this kind of risk. The aim is to invest in different types of assets so that they won't all be affected in the same manner.

For instance, let us say that you have a portfolio that consists of solely airline stocks. If it is announced that all the pilots are going on a strike and that the flights will be canceled, then the value of your investments will drop. However, had you diversified your portfolio and made an investment in some railway stocks as well, then only a part of your portfolio would have suffered. In fact, there is a chance that the prices of your railway stock would have increased as the prices of the airline stock decreased. You could diversify your portfolio further since there are risks that affect aviation and railway industries.

To achieve better diversification, you could diversify not only into different types of companies but also into different types of industries. Let your stocks be uncorrelated. It is also important that you start diversifying among the different classes of assets. Different assets react to the same situation in different ways. Stocks wouldn't react the way bonds would, and vice versa. A combination of assets will help in spreading the risk and also in reducing the portfolio's sensitivity towards unfavorable market conditions.

The markets of bonds and equities tend to move in different directions. Thus, a diversified portfolio will help in setting off the loss from one unpleasant market movement against a favorable one. Even the best analysis of the financial statements of a company doesn't guarantee that the investment wouldn't be a losing one. Diversification won't prevent the loss. However, it can help reduce the impact of the loss and reduce the risk borne by you.

The next question would be regarding the number of stocks that you should hold. Owning five stocks would certainly be better than holding on to one. However, there comes a point after which it doesn't make any sense to keep on adding more stock to your portfolio.

There is a debate about the number of stocks that you will need to reduce the risk while maintaining a good return. The most conventional school of thought suggests owning between 15 and 20 stocks that are spread across various industries. Diversification can definitely help an investor in managing the risk and in reducing the volatility of an instrument. The caveat that needs to be remembered is that regardless of how diversified your portfolio is, you can never fully eliminate risk altogether. All you can do is to try and reduce the risk that is associated with different individual stocks.

However, the general market conditions tend to have an impact on all the stocks available. Therefore, it is important to diversify into different classes of assets as well. The key is to find the perfect balance between the risk and returns expected while keeping in mind your financial goals.

Building the Perfect Portfolio

When compared to individual stock picking, a well-balanced portfolio would certainly have a better long-term impact on overall performance. Picking stocks is fun when compared to thinking about asset allocation and the percentage of stocks that you should hold. There are a couple of rules that you should follow so that the process of building your portfolio won't be difficult. Here are the rules that you should take into consideration:

Your Goals

Knowing your goals will help you get started – when you will need the money, the amount, and how soon you need it. When you start saving for a long-term goal, time can help in smoothening over the returns from any volatile instrument. When you are holding on to more volatile assets, a long-term perspective helps.

Volatility refers to any ups and downs in the market price of an asset. However, a volatile investment wouldn't work in your favor while you are saving for a short-term purpose. The chances of such an investment plummeting are quite high. If you are living off a fixed income, then you should be watchful of the damage that inflation can do. Having diversified investments helps in reducing the blow of inflation.

Take your risk Tolerance into Consideration

All sorts of investments have got some risk involved. Even the ones that seem "safe," like treasury bonds and blue chip stocks, tend to have some risk involved. If you are in need of some money for a short-term goal and cannot afford to lose any money, then the best option available to you would be a product insured by FDIC, like a savings account or a CD (Certificate of Deposit). The riskier the asset tends to be, the higher the returns are. The high risk involved makes these investments extremely volatile. You will need to decide on the proportion in which you would like to hold your investments and the ratio of risky investments to less risky investments. You get to decide this ratio depending on your goals and needs.

There are more than just stocks and bonds. You can invest in more than one type of asset. One way in which you can reduce volatility is by doing this. You need to add some alternative assets, such as commodities or even real estate, to your portfolio. Commodities can help counteract the effects of inflation. This happens because the prices of commodities tend to shoot up during inflation.

If you are averse to taking any risks, then you should seriously consider investing in a fund that is market neutral – something that would aim at making a profit regardless of whether the market is bullish or bearish. Even if the values of your investments, like houses, precious artifacts, and other valuables, haven't been updated in the quarterly brokerage statement, you should know the value of your investment portfolio. Even if such items aren't sold off easily, their value and associated risks need to be taken into consideration before you think of expanding your portfolio.

There are a couple of things that you shouldn't do while you are putting together your investment portfolio. Most investors tend to make the several mistakes. Your investment shouldn't be based on a fad. If you start investing based on a fad, then it is very likely that it will not head in the right direction. It is more than likely that the investment has already produced good results even before you got to know about it. The "set it and forget it" mentality will cost you in investing.

You will have to keep reviewing your portfolio on a regular basis. You will need to keep diversifying, and change your pattern of asset allocation for risk mitigation. It takes a long time to make up for any setback that your portfolio might have encountered, so be thorough in your research before you decide to make an investment.

Alan Anderson

Key Highlights

The very first thing to remember before entering the stock market is to thoroughly understand what it stands for. Not having proper knowledge on the subject can cause you to make errors of judgment. This means that you will end up choosing the wrong options for yourself without knowing how you will be rewarded for it. The first chapter of this book provided you with ample information on the basics of stock markets and the different concepts that govern it. You must go through it twice or thrice to understand all the concepts well enough.

You must be well aware that there are many types of markets and investors that exist in this world. You have to get well acquainted with each type and understand their true nature. This will give you the chance to decide on the type of investor that you would like to be. The basic choices include fundamentalists and contrarians. A fundamentalist is someone who goes through all the basics of the company and understands everything about its profit and loss, progress, reports, dividends, etc. A contrarian, on the other hand, will not be interested in the functioning of the company and will only look at the company's share prices and move against the crowd.

There are different ways to figure out whether the stock option is profitable. Some methods involve mathematical equations, while others seek out patterns and graphs. It is important to find a system that works for you and your investment needs. Some methods do not work well with different investments, while in some cases, the opposite is true. There are methods that work perfectly with certain types of investments. For example, the candlestick chart is great for intraday traders, as they will see how the stock is doing over a period time and decide how they will proceed by selling or buying stock.

The first type of share market investment to consider is stocks. Stocks are a great investment choice for all the beginners out there. The stock market helps put out several options to choose from, and it is best to follow it sector-wise. There are several sectors, including IT, finance, banking, fast moving consumer goods, etc. You can choose two good stocks from each sector and follow them for a month to understand how they operate. After you understand everything, you can start investing in them.

It is also important to remember that you should invest in stocks from companies that you have actually heard of when you first start investing. This way, you are playing it safe, as these stocks are generally not risky. However, it is advised that you do not invest in social media stock initially, as the stock tends to very risky because many of these companies are have a short life span that usually lasts less than 15 years. However, if you must invest in a company that owns any social media platforms, then play it safe, and invest in Google or Yahoo.

When it comes to stocks, you should always research the company to see if it is worth your investment as you want to minimize any risks with stocks. If it looks like the company has been losing money for a long period of time, do not invest in the company's stocks.

There are two types of trades that take place in the stock market, one being long-term investments and the other being short-term investments. Long-term investments are held for a minimum of five years and can go up to 10 or more years. The investor is interested in the dividend that the company pays to its shareholders. An example of a long-term investment is bonds. Bonds should not be sold until they reach maturity as the bonds will not be worth much until then. As the bond matures, investors are paid dividends by the issuer. On the other hand, short-term investments are those where the investor tries to capitalize on the difference in share values. Say you bought a share for $50 face value and sold it after a month for $100. You will arrive at a profit from it. There is no role for dividend here.

Like stocks, you can choose options for yourself. Options are like stocks, but they come with some leeway. You have the choice of paying for the stocks in full after a few weeks' time, before which you only pay an advance to reserve the stock. This type is a better choice than buying the stock outright. The rate of interest here will be much higher, and you will have the chance to increase the return that you receive on your investment. With options, you have to remember that they expire after a certain period of time. American options are more flexible than European options. While options may not be as flexible as stocks, they are still a better choice as there are fewer risks involved.

Just like options, there is another future security that you can trade in, and it is known as commodities. These commodities are traded in the market on a daily basis. Their prices will never remain constant and will keep changing from time to time. If you wish to trade in the commodities market, then you must keep an eye on the prices, as they will change on a minute-to-minute basis. Moreover, the money involved in this type of trade is quite high.

There are different kinds of commodities that someone can invest in. These include livestock, energy, and metals. Metal is the most interesting commodity, as it includes both precious and non-precious metals in the market. This is the kind of trade in which an investor will hire a high-end broker that usually has a research team at his or her fingertips, which mean that he or she can keep track of the minute changes in commodities. Although there are different ways to trade metals outside commodities, similar to stocks and bonds, those options are not as safe as commodities.

If the stock market is not your first choice for investments, then you can also choose the bond market. Bonds are issued by the government and are seen as safer choices to make. You will not have a high credit risk, which means that you will almost always get back your entire investment, along with an interest rate. However, the interest that these bonds pay will not be as high as those from other forms of investment. However, the safety factor is what draws people to bonds, and you can choose them if you are concerned about your money's safety. However, if the government did not receive enough income from taxes, they will borrow money to pay the bondholders. This can lead to an economic crisis that will affect the stock market because most people will try to save money and not take any risks. The stock market is one great risk.

Just like government bonds, corporations also issue bonds. These corporate bonds are better options for you if you are looking to increase your investment over the course of time. They will pay you a higher rate of interest, and you can double or triple your investment. The risk, however, is extremely high. You might not get your money back in full, or you might not get any part of it. Most investors don't look at this aspect, as the companies always deliver on their promise. You have to check the fundamentals of the company to see if they are capable of paying you back your money in full. In this case, it is very important that you research everything you can about the corporation issuing your bond. However, it is the risk you pay for investing money in a risky venture like a corporate bond.

The next type of investment that you can choose is known as mutual funds. These are another form of high-risk, high-reward investments. You can invest in a mutual fund for three to five years. When you invest in a mutual fund, you don't have the right to choose where your money goes, so you will have to settle for whatever that your mutual fund manager chooses for you. You can check your net asset value at the end of each day, and check how your investments are faring. There are many types of mutual fund investments to choose from.

However, in the case of insurance, there are two types of investments: the stock and the mutual fund. The reason is that there are two types of insurance companies. You have companies like Progressive and MetLife, which enable people to buy stocks in the marketplace that are called insurance shares. The companies involved are members of the stock exchanges, and anyone can buy or sell their stock. However, the insurance shares are long-term investments, so they are not for everyone. You can make a profit from them due to dividends. A mutual company, like Liberty Mutual, is a policyholder owned fund, so if you do not have a policy from that insurance company, you cannot own shares. These shares are paid for by the premiums that policyholders pay, but the policyholders get their returns either by dividends or lower premium payments. If for some reason, a mutual company has a rise in expenses that premium payments cannot cover, then the company can become an insurance share, and the policyholders become investors.

(clearing)

ETFs stand for exchange-traded funds. As the name suggests, these are funds that are traded on the exchange. If you are to invest in mutual funds, you will have to wait for a long time before they mature. However, an ETF is like a mutual fund that is traded on a regular basis on the stock market, such that you have the chance to buy and sell the entire gamut of investment at the same time. The other advantage is that the fees you pay towards your broker will be much lower than what you will pay your mutual fund manager.

There are many different types of ETF investments. These investments include foreign currency, sector and industry, and volatility. These types of investments are great for having a diverse portfolio. ETF is similar to ETN, which is short for exchanged traded note, as they are both traded on major stock exchanges and track assets. However, ETNs are more like bonds that are issued by banks and not by the government or government-approved entities. ETN are riskier than ETF investments because if anything happens to the bank, whether it is bankruptcy or a credit rating downgrade, it affects the bond and the investor either by defaulting on the investor or lowering the market price of the bond.

Precious metals are great investments that you can choose. These metals will only grow in value over time, and you will have the chance to sell them anywhere globally and get the same price everywhere. You will also gain immediate possession of your investment, and you don't have to wait for the certificates to be published. You can also convert these metals into jewelry and still remain in profit.

There are many precious metals to choose from, and you can choose the one that you think will best suit your portfolio. The best investment for precious metals is an ETF, as you can avoid the many fees and taxes associated with precious metals.

For example, if you have invested in gold, and you wanted it sent to your house, you would have to pay a duty tax, a service tax, and a wealth tax. However, if you have a gold ETF, you would avoid paying these taxes. Although manager fees are expensive, there are fewer taxes. So it will be up to you in this hypothetical situation to determine which is more important: paying a higher commission fee or paying three different taxes on one item.

Social media stocks, while extremely risky, might become a very huge market in the future, as most of us use social media platforms for numerous reasons – be it personal or professional. The stocks are very popular right now and are somewhat easy to understand. Profits are dependent on user growth; however, many of these platforms have a short life span, as users will eventually move on to another website or app if the platform does not adapt to the needs of the many. In some cases, adapting the need for the few has caused user growth to decline, but the companies actually lost users. Nevertheless, researching social media stock can help you decide if this investment is suited to you.

Lastly, brokers are one of the most important aspects of investing. Brokers can help you with investments and other financial advice associated with your investments. There are many types of brokers that can help you with your portfolio. It is important to remember that brokers have licenses, and brokerages are members of regulatory organizations. Such information is useful if you plan on using online brokers. It can help you determine whether the firms are real or not. Despite the fees entailed by the use of brokers, they help you invest money and can keep track of your portfolio for you.

It is always important to avoid investing into things you do not understand. This might be the most important rule in investing. It does not matter if your broker thinks that a certain investment is a great idea. You should research the investment first, and if you still don't understand it, then don't waste your money. For example, if you broker wants you to invest in foreign currency but you do not understand how that will work, then you should research the different types of funds, stocks, etc., associated with foreign currency, and if you still do not get it, tell your broker that you don't want to invest in it no matter how great it is for your portfolio. This kind of situation can happen to anyone, but it is your money, and minimizing risks is always a great idea in investment.

Hopefully, all this information can help you find what investments are best for you.

Conclusion

Thank you, once again, for choosing this book.

The main aim of this book was to educate you on the topic of portfolio investments. Remember that your portfolio should be diverse, and you must try and invest a little in all types of options. Concentrating on just one type might not give you the desired returns on your investment.

Once you gain confidence, you will start to deal with ease and not worry about incurring losses. You will understand that it is part and parcel of the trade. I hope you find success in your portfolio investment endeavors.

Finally, I'd like to ask you a favor, if I may. If you enjoyed this book, then I'd really appreciate you leaving a review and your feedback on Amazon.

All the best!

Alan Anderson

TODAY IS THE DAY, TAKE CHARGE OF YOUR TEAM!

The idea behind writing this book was to use my experience to help those starting out and to be able to give useful and sound advice. There are many corporate style books on leadership. What makes mine different is that it's written by someone who has been where you are currently standing, and who understands your difficulty with being faced with the job of team leader for the first time. Walk through the pages and learn how it's done. It's actually easier than you may imagine, once you know what it is that you need to be doing.

In this book you will learn how to:
- Effectively communicate with your team
- Allocate and delegate
- Identify your teams strengths and weaknesses
- Develop your coaching skills
- Manage conflict resolution
- Improve your coaching skills
- Become a great leader
- And much, much more

Visit to Order Your Copy Today!
www.amazon.com/gp/product/B011S5Y4F2